If It's Shreveport, It Must Be Tuesday

Also by Marilyn Carr

How I Invented the Internet

Nowhere like This Place: Tales from a Nuclear Childhood

Praise for *How I Invented the Internet*

"Excellent writing, with humour tucked in all over the place. Marilyn has exceeded her writing skills in her second amazing book. I highly recommend anyone to read it, especially those of us who grew to adulthood in the '70s, '80s and '90s. Just loved it!" —Amazon.com

"*How I Invented the Internet* picks up where *Nowhere Like This Place* left off, following Marilyn Carr as a newly minted library science graduate sprung from the confines of the scientifically-cultured-yet-culturally-cloistered town of Deep River and relocated to the yuppiedom of Toronto in the 1980s. Carr makes the terrain of working woman in the era seem appealing and disheartening in equal measure as she recounts navigating mostly-male workplaces, stalker ex-boyfriends, and home-invading vermin with fly-by-the-seat-of-her-pants gumption and ingenuity." —Goodreads.com

"The author has a unique gift for conveying ideas and imagery through thoughtfully crafted wording, employing a variety of literary devices to draw the reader in and make them a part of the story. I trust she will continue in her endeavours and leave us entertained for many more reads to come." —Chaptersindigo.ca

Praise for *Nowhere like This Place*

"What do you get when you transplant a young girl from Quebec into what could arguably be called the most unique community in all of Canada in the 1960s and watch her grow up there? You get the makings of a very funny and perspective book." —*North Renfrew Times*

"A coming-of-age book like no other. How could life be normal in a town that wasn't? Carr manages to make you feel like you are there with her, wending her way through a "manufactured" town where, much like *Alice in Wonderland*, nothing is quite as it seems. Carr's comfort with words is obvious as she helps us laugh along with her descriptions of a childhood and adolescence that we can all relate to. A funny and thoroughly enjoyable read." —Goodreads.com

"Marilyn Carr's writing style is fluid and laced with a wry sense of humour that was a delight to read. You come away with a sense of knowing the author as if you had been friends for years. It's an outstanding book and a must read for anyone seeking a journey back to their time of youth." —Chaptersindigo.com

If It's Shreveport, It Must Be Tuesday

Based on a True Story

MARILYN CARR

IGUANA

Copyright © 2025 Marilyn Carr
Published by Iguana Books
720 Bathurst Street
Toronto, ON M5S 2R4

All rights reserved. No part of this publication may be reproduced, stored in a retrieval system or transmitted, in any form or by any means, electronic, mechanical, recording or otherwise (except brief passages for purposes of review) without the prior permission of the author.

Publisher: Cheryl Hawley
Front cover design: Jonathan Relph

ISBN 978-1-77180-741-8 (paperback)
ISBN 978-1-77180-740-1 (epub)

This is an original print edition of *If It's Shreveport, It Must Be Tuesday*.

For everyone who has ever been a stranger in a strange land.

1

As I scarf down some yogurt to fuel my bike ride to work, I scan the front page of *The Globe and Mail* business section. The ashes of the dotcom meltdown are clearly still smoldering. Tech companies, both dubious and formerly stalwart enterprises, are being torched and scorched on a regular basis, even in 2001. *Interest rates back up to 8%! The NASDAQ closes at all time low!* The G&M informs me in full sky-is-falling mode. The inside pages are no better. Unemployment is up. Housing is a buyer's market. The world didn't end almost a year and a half ago when the calendar page flipped over to January 1, 2000, but clearly all is not well.

But enough perusing the paper. I need to get to work. I'm already dressed in a t-shirt and gym shorts, so all I need to do is stuff my more presentable clothes into a pannier bag and clip it onto the back of my blue Miele — my beater hybrid that lives in the front hall. When my parents visited to see my post-divorce house a couple of months ago, my mother observed, "Does your bike really need to be in the front hall? In the winter? Who rides a bike in the winter?" Yes, it does. And *I* do. My bike is my sole mode of wheeled transportation and it would be a major inconvenience if it were stolen, which has happened many times. Okay, not to this particular bike (yet), but to seven of its long-lost brethren.

There's no need for a car because everything is in walking and biking distance. I do have a driver's licence, which I finally obtained at thirty on a dare, but its only job is to serve as ID. I haven't been behind a wheel since I passed the test twelve years ago. My ex-husband used to say I was only a marginally better passenger than driver, which I think is uncharitable. But, also, completely true.

I'm the third owner of my house since 1901. Little old lady died, little old lady died, then me: little-ish at five-foot four and barely clearing a hundred pounds, but by no means *old*, even though I'm on the wrong side of forty. The last time it was renovated was in 1955, with all the mod cons and colour choices that implies. The stove looks like it belongs in *The Honeymooners* kitchen and the pee-coloured Formica on the countertop has burn marks from several decades of misplaced pots and pans and countless knife knicks from what I assume were enthusiastic dinner preparations. The house needs everything done to it you can imagine and probably things that defy imagination.

Some HVAC guys are coming by after work to tell me what it will cost to replace the boiler and the two oil tanks (two oil tanks!!) that fuel it and get rid of the heavier-than-anvils cast iron radiators. At least I have a well-paying job with the promise of a hefty bonus when our fiscal year ends in September.

I cram my red hair into my helmet, heft my bike out the door and down the peeling wooden stairs of a sad porch that leans to the left, then wheel it along the cracked concrete of the front walkway. My route to work takes me due south and downhill on Broadview, west on Queen Street to where it forks with King, then left on Yonge all the way to the lake. It's a pleasant ride and I use the time to muse idly about the day ahead. Likely the same old. Check email and voicemail, usually sparse and inconsequential. The weekly status meeting is at ten o'clock. I'll need to come up with a list of things I've done that sound meaningful and productive. Lunch at noon. Afternoon spent shuffling papers. I never thought working at a tech start-up could be so boring. But I can't quibble with the paycheque.

When I arrive at One Yonge Street, I'm lucky to find an empty spot in the bike rack that's closest to the front door. I unclip my pannier, release my Kryptonite U-lock from its holder on the frame, and secure the bike to the post. I take off my helmet but bring it with me as I walk up the steps to the front door. I don't think helmets are stolen very often, but I like this one and it fits well, so I don't want to take a chance. It has a kind of swirly black-on-white thing going on and I bought a kid's size so it would fit what my helpful friends call my "pin head." Come to think of it, any normal adult wouldn't be able to wear it, so I'm not sure why I'm so careful with it. Maybe because carting a bike helmet around makes me look like the urban street warrior I aspire to be seen as. Not the business school graduate, debt-laden yuppie that I am.

I snag just a snippet of conversation from the guy who gets off the elevator as I enter at seven forty-five. "Missed third-round funding," I think he said. He probably saw the same article I read this morning about the sad plight of tech companies. I press the button for the twenty-fourth floor. The corridor is empty as I leave the elevator car and so is the handicapped bathroom that I use as my change room. I strip off my bike shorts and t-shirt, sop up my glow with paper towel, and change into an outfit appropriate for a start-up: ombre-striped matching shell and cardigan in decreasing shades of pink. Op art flowered miniskirt. Birkenstocks.

Maxlink, where I work, is a nascent telecom company whose mission is to supply the "last-mile internet" to low-rent office buildings. This is going to be accomplished by satellites and thin air. No need for costly infrastructure upgrades! Class C buildings will be able to charge Class B rent! Or something like that. I started here in January, four months ago, to be in charge of documenting business processes so the company will look like it has its act together, so investors will invest. Our office does indeed look impressive from the outside. In the marble-clad reception room a well-groomed twenty-something, wearing a geometric-patterned Diane von Furstenberg knock-off wrap dress, murmurs quietly into a phone. She's probably arranging a manicure appointment or rallying her BFFs for Friday cocktails, not intercepting an important call. Because it's not only my phone that rarely rings.

2

Once I pass through the glass doors to the inner sanctum, the ambience devolves into a rat-maze of intersecting cubicles. As a holder of a fancy job title — Director of Process Improvement — I get a semblance of an office. I don't exactly have a window but more of what a real estate agent would call a "window view," as there is a narrow hallway separating my door from the floor-to-ceiling glass. When my door is open, I can see the Toronto Islands and the condo that's right next door, within spitting distance. So close that the guys congregate every afternoon to watch the clean-freak lady on the twenty-fourth floor who vacuums every day at three o'clock. Completely naked. I guess they need to derive excitement from something, because it sure isn't available within these walls.

I enter my enclave, fling my pannier on my visitor chair and boot up my computer. I am almost logged into email when Serge bustles in. He's a short, roundish, jolly, Quebec French guy. We got hired because Normand, the CIO, knew us from the consulting firm we both used to work for. I didn't know Serge before I got here because he worked in the Montreal office and I was in Toronto, but we've become fast friends because we speak the same language: consulting firm lingo. We speak of methodologies and deliverables and decks and use-cases and entities.

Maxlink uses a lot of consultants, including a big crew from our old firm, which was recently sold to IBM, most of whom get billed to us at a thousand dollars a day. Serge's job is to oversee the projects the consultants are working on. He gets to boss ex-colleagues around and make them accountable for their billables. We both enjoy this a little more than would seem appropriate, but then again, the meaning of appropriate kind of flies out the window when you work for a tech start-up.

We've compared notes and Normand apparently gave us both the same smooth sales pitch, complete with copious exclamatory sentences. "It's a start-up, so you can write your own ticket! Invent your own role! It's telecom, a bullet-proof industry! The need for internet connections is exploding! The mainstream providers can't keep up! You can pretty much name your price and there'll be stock options very soon!" he said.

I'm guessing he made a bunch of big promises to broker himself a good package and needed us to make them happen. But the job I had at the time at a niche consulting business that never seemed to have more than one client was not looking promising. At least this sounded more exciting. I couldn't resist those enthusiastic exclamation points. I bit.

Serge eyes my pannier and raises his eyebrows. I sigh and move it from the chair to the gap between my desk and the wall. He plops into the guest chair. "Did you see the email?" he asks.

"No. I just got here. I'll log in once I check my voicemail."

"Don't bother logging in. It may not work anyhow. We just got notified that round three funding is toast. We are probably toast. Or as we would say in French, *nous sommes brioche*. There's an all-hands meeting in half an hour. Let's grab a coffee first. Oh. Right. Tea for you."

We head down to the cafeteria and nab a booth by the window. There are already some sailboats out on Lake Ontario this early in the season, serenely wafting in the wind. I am definitely not serene nor even close to calmly wafting. "I don't know what I'll do if we're going under," I say. "My resume reads like a list of ghost companies. How is it I could have worked for five companies — so far — that got acquired and disappeared? Then the companies that acquired them eventually realized they didn't really get anything when they bought a professional services company and got rid of most of the staff they inherited. Anybody who reads my CV is going to think I'm either an idiot or a jinx. Or probably both. The only reason I got hired here is that Normand knew me and my expertise. If Maxlink is toast, I am toast."

Serge does look serene as he sips his espresso. "Let's just wait to see what they say at the meeting. Maybe we'll get a good severance package. If I start day-trading full time, I could parlay it into a small fortune in a couple of months. I can work for myself and not have to rely on anyone else. You should try it too!"

"You don't have a two-hundred-and-fifty-thousand-dollar mortgage. You just rent. You could also move back to Montreal where it's cheaper. I can't take a risk like that. I'd need to find a blue-chip full-time job. Maybe I should go back and work for a bank. Or an oil company. You don't see them going bust."

We take the elevator up to the empty space on the twenty-third floor, which was earmarked for the telecom operations room, which has yet to show any sign of existing. There are no chairs, just standing room, and there's a computer projector on a table at the front, aimed at the blank wall. Everyone's in a huddle with their department cohort. Serge and I claim a patch of floor near the back.

The clutches of groups split apart and remerge as Joel, the CEO and company founder, walks through the room followed by his assistant Ewan, who wears the requisite hoodie and Maxlink logoed t-shirt. Nothing happens for a few minutes while Ewan boots up a laptop and turns on the projector. The room is mostly silent while we wait, but it pulses with an undercurrent of both trepidation and anticipation. Maybe we're all going to get those stock options Normand dangled or a special quarterly bonus. Maybe I'm delusional.

3

Not many of us have ever seen Joel, as he spends most of his time out of the office, wheeling and dealing, or whatever tech CEOs do during working hours. He's in his early fifties and wears rimless glasses and a Hugo Boss suit, although his blue shirt is tieless and unbuttoned at the neck. His manicured hands are completely empty, and he stares blankly over our heads as he waits for his assistant to do his thing. As if there are no other humans in the room. This is not a surprise because, if the scuttlebutt is true, Joel thinks he's above all of us mere mortals.

The wall now displays a PowerPoint slide. It has lots of red numbers and a graph that's the reverse of the coveted hockey stick revenue curve that rises exponentially to the heavens. Maxlink is clearly headed in the other direction. In a hand basket. "As you may know, our first two rounds of funding went very well. Just under fifty million dollars," Joel says. "That gave us great confidence our third round would attract even more interest. It appears that confidence may have been somewhat misplaced. At our burn rate of one million a week, we are out of money by midnight. We will be in receivership as of tomorrow. Today will be our last payroll. Thank you for your service. You may leave your keys with reception." In other words, don't let the door hit you on the way out. And with that, he leaves the room.

The rest of us do the same. Serge and I trudge up the dismal concrete stairwell rather than wait for several elevator loads. When we arrive at our section of the twenty-fourth floor, Normand is waiting. He is tall, with a distinguished grey mustache and always wears a suit as impeccable as Joel's, maybe as armour to stave off the hoodied start-up anarchy. He waves Serge and me into his windowed corner office. I guess he had already heard the message. "Well, that didn't work out so well," he says. "But look on the bright side. We are now free to do whatever we want, like take the summer off. I'm going to sail every day. Maybe down to the Caribbean." Easy for him to say. I leave Serge and Normand having a lively discussion in French, likely about the silver lining they've decided they just got handed.

I gather up my meagre belongings and stuff them in my pannier. A few pens and some notebooks. Two pairs of shoes from under the desk. I take one last look out the window at the lake, where dark clouds are gathering over the Toronto Islands. The elevator is full but silent as we descend. There was talk of heading to the sports bar next door, but I'd rather go home.

I walk toward the bike racks and can see the two bikes I parked next to, but not mine. When I get closer, I see part of my bike — the back wheel. Still locked to the post. *Thank you, universe, for piling on.* I detach the lock and jam it into the pannier, a hundred bucks apparently not well spent. I debate whether or not to harvest the wheel but what good would it do? Plus, now I have to take the subway home and I already have the heavy pannier and my helmet to carry. The wheel stays behind as a cautionary tale for other bike commuters.

As I head north up Yonge Street to King station, big fat drops start to hit the sidewalk, and the sky gets much darker. A celestial power failure. I pick up my pace but I'm not fast enough to reach the overhead shelter of the Gardiner Expressway before it starts to pelt rain. Then hail. No silver lining in my cloud, evidently. I wait out the worst of it, but since I'm already so saturated that more water wouldn't make a difference, I resume my trek to the subway. Drenched, despondent, and dejected.

I board the subway train in my sopping spandex with my soggy pannier, dripping in the doorway to avoid the side-eye of the passengers who are clearly not encouraging me to claim the empty seat in the middle of the car. Only eight stops and one interchange 'til I'm home and dry and get to find out what the HVAC is going to cost. Tomorrow, I'll have to dust off my Rolodex and start dialling for dollars.

4

"Didn't you hear?" says my friend Paul at Imperial Oil. "They've moved head office to Calgary. We're winding down Toronto. Unless you want to move, no jobs here. How are you doing, anyway?" Not good, Paul. Not good.

"Didn't you hear?" says my friend Patricia at the Canadian Imperial Bank of Commerce. "The executive briefing book is now fully automated. It only takes two of us to support it. There's even a new document management system, so every department is downsizing. How are you doing anyway?" I've been better, Patricia. I've been better.

"Didn't you hear?" says my friend Tim at Brown & Associates. "Things are completely off the rails since we got acquired by IBM. Even management has to be eighty percent billable. People are getting kicked to the curb left, right, and centre. How are you doing anyway?" Worse every minute, Tim. Can things actually get any worse?

"Didn't you hear?" says my friend Arnold at Serendipity Partners. "We just got bought by a private equity firm. Fred and Bruce are taking the money and running. The rest of us are being thrown to the Wall Street wolves. How are you doing anyway?" Bad doesn't begin to describe it, Arnold. Bad is not a good enough word.

"Didn't you hear?" says my friend Mel at Hydro One. "They've decided to sell the Bruce nuclear plant to the private sector. There's a hiring and spending freeze until the deal closes. I can't even requisition a pencil! How are you doing anyway?" Utterly despondent, Mel. I have nothing else to say.

I decide to give my finger and phone a rest. Or maybe I can stomach one last call before I start applying for welfare.

"Didn't you hear?" says my friend Sue, who used to work at Brown & Associates and is now at a company called BDE. "I'm taking a sabbatical. But who knows? There might be some stuff that needs doing while I'm away. I'll get back to you. How are you doing anyway?" Watching money be incinerated by my new furnace, Sue. And it hasn't even been installed yet.

The space I've set up as an office on the third floor of my house is basic but works for me. The desk is an IKEA kitchen table that has been from Toronto to Saskatoon and back and has survived being painted red then green, a transformation that is unfortunately obvious given my lack of painting skills. There's a phone and my laptop and a computer modem and a bunch of notebooks. An assortment of pens sits in a mug that has a *Cathy* cartoon on the front. Almost half of them work.

I'm determined not to get a job at any more tech companies, since the industry seems intent on imploding. I need something more stable. Maybe in an industry I've never tried. Like fast food restaurants or education or accounting. My modem beeps through the dial-up phone number and the outer space noise tells me it's connected. I start my job search at Dogpile because it covers all the engines, including Yahoo!, AltaVista, WebCrawler, HotBot, and Excite. I notice the irony. If I hadn't worked so long in tech, I wouldn't know about Dogpile and I probably wouldn't even have a modem in my house. My literacy is hopefully going to make it much easier to find a job that's as far removed from the technology sector as possible. I scroll through job postings on Workopolis. So far, the options are both dismal and bizarre.

General Manager, Poultry Insurance Exchange. Maybe a Poultry Insurance Exchange operates kind of like the stock exchange. If you are a turkey, for example, you would want extra insurance in October and December (and possibly in the spring), but for the rest of the time, it wouldn't be as important. What you would do is list your insurance policy on the Poultry Insurance Exchange in the off-seasons so that some others of the fowl persuasion could pay you a fee to use it. Surely that's the explanation.

Director, Communicable Diseases. I really hope this job pays a lot, because you would have to be on duty 24-7. I am sure there is a new instance of a communicable disease wreaking havoc on someone every waking (or even sleeping) second. However, I'm glad to know that someone is watching our backs, at least if there is a twenty-first century Florence Nightingale out there willing to step up to the plate. Definitely not me.

Regional Director, Retirement. Up until now, I had no idea that there would be someone out there to make sure my retirement was properly directed. I am a little unclear about the scope of this service. Is it mandatory or optional? Does it cover leisure activities or focus on things oldsters might do to fill their time in a meaningful way? I will never know.

I hang up the modem to contemplate who I should call next to beg for a job. As if the phone reads my mind, it rings as soon as I disconnect from the internet.

"This is Simon Brown from BDE. Your friend Sue gave me your name," the person on the other end says. "I'm glad I finally got through. I was beginning to think I had the wrong number because the line's been busy for hours." Thank you, useless job search. But isn't BDE a tech company? Didn't I just vow to get out of tech? I never intended to get into it in the first place. I'm cursed.

"Hi, Simon," I say. "What's up?"

"I need some help with a project," he says. "Sue said you would be perfect." I ask him to tell me what he has in mind. "You probably know that BDE — Big Data Enterprises — is a global technology market analyst firm. What makes us special is data is literally our middle name. Unlike other analyst firms whose names I will not sully my lips by mentioning, we base all our analysis and recommendations on rigorous primary and secondary research. It's all about stats, correlations, and causations," he says.

I had a brief relationship with statistics in business school and it did not end well. Neither does it seem this conversation will end well. "So, we're about to launch a syndicated qualitative multi-client study," Simon says. "And I need some feet on the ground." I am tempted to pretend I understand what he's talking about, but since I am not yet sure if I have nothing invested or everything invested, I ask Simon to please back up and explain what a multi-client is.

"So, at BDE we make money a few ways. We sell subscriptions to our regular reports, we do custom research projects for customers, and we do multi-clients. For those, we get a bunch of technology companies to sponsor a study and the whole group gets the results. It's pretty lucrative because we do the research and analysis once, but sell it for big bucks multiple times," he says. He tells me this particular multi-client is a little different than usual because it involves executive interviews instead of survey research. It's a study to determine whether or not (and fingers crossed not "or not") companies that have the software that runs the nuts and bolts of their business hosted remotely at an application service provider get a good return on their investment.

Now I know why Sue thinks I can do this job. Application service providers (ASPs) are the early twenty-first century's version of computer time-sharing. Back in the eighties, computer time-sharing was a thing where businesses rented the horsepower of mainframe computers from a time-sharing company because it was too expensive to have their own. My very first job was with a computer time-sharing company. I didn't really have much to do with delivering the actual sharing of computer time, all I did was upload software updates and keep track of versions. But that is not information Simon needs to know. I decide it's worth finding out more.

5

Hi, it's your team calling. You on for NTN tonight? We're going to be down at Scotland Yard.

My friend Josh's voice is on the machine. I can't think of a reason not to go play trivia, except that Scotland Yard isn't as handy as it used to be now that I'm not working at One Yonge Street. But then again, I don't think he knows that yet.

The King streetcar drops me off at Church Street and from there it's a couple of blocks' walk south to The Esplanade. I enter the dim bar and head toward the nook in the corner where we always sit. The lack of light does a big favour to the décor. The pub has only been around for about twenty years, but it's done up to look like it was born in England in the middle of the last century. Even though it's a while since smoking was banned in restaurants, the tin ceilings are nicotine yellow. Dark-green wooden wainscotting, scratched and nicked by previous patrons, encloses one side of the booths and the swirly red carpet is frayed under the tables, where countless shoes have rested on it.

The usual crowd is here: Josh, Len, and Howard. I met them all when I worked at a consulting firm, and to amuse ourselves after work, we would play trivia once a week at a bar near the office. NTN's an interactive game. They beam questions to a screen in a bar and you answer using a keypad. We compete with people all across North America and win fabulous prizes — if you count free beer as fabulous. My handle is Elvis. It used to be Not Dead Elvis, but I shortened it. It's an incredibly funny joke about Elvis being out there somewhere, playing trivia. You had to be there, I guess. The guys all play as rodents: Weasel, Stoat, and Ferret. There was a clever reason for this at one point, but we've all forgotten what it was. Probably something about being evil and treacherous. And carnivorous. I watch Josh attack his burger, cooked rare. Definitely carnivorous.

There are usually the same people playing every Tuesday, poised to oppose our North American domination. The leader board shows our immediate competition right now, but when the game goes live, we'll see the list of competitors from across the continent who dare to vie for our position in the top ten.

"Did I tell you guys my company went under? I am toast," I say.

"Well, that's what you get for working at a start-up," says Howard. "I bet they promised you stock options so they could pay you less than you deserve. Oh. But I guess paying you less is better than not paying you at all. Me, I've got a defined benefit pension where I work now. And of course, the golden handcuffs to go along with it. I keep a calendar at my desk and cross off the days until retirement. Only 5,982 to go." Howard got a job at a bank a year ago. I had a job at a bank once. It was as stifling and soul-sucking as it appears Howard's job is. On the plus side, he has a job and the bank isn't likely to go under for lack of funds.

"I wouldn't want to be unemployed right now. After all the Y2K work dried up, there were a lot of programmers looking around. I think IT's in a slump," says Josh. "And don't you need lots of work done on that derelict house you bought? Sucks to be you." Josh always tells it like it is. He's the kind of guy who exclusively wears ironic t-shirts. Today's shirt even says *I.ron.ic — Adjective* followed by a list of supposed ironies from

Alanis's famous song, including the rain, free ride, and good advice. I've never been convinced that these classify as actual ironies. Seems to me they're just bad luck or bad timing.

Regardless, in response to his shirt, I say "I would take your advice, Josh, if you had any. Or if it was actually good."

Then Len weighs in. Len doesn't just see all glasses as half empty, I'm not sure if he even believes he owns a glass. He looks as risk averse as he is, with a polo shirt that has a starched collar and jeans that don't have a hint of fade in the denim. If his girlfriend would let him, he'd be wearing both a belt and suspenders. "Do you have a bundle buggy? It's almost summer. You could always camp out in the park when the bank repossesses your house. Or maybe an even better approach would be to buy a gun and a bullet, and when you run out of money, it's *hasta la vista*, baby!"

"Wouldn't it be better to buy more than one bullet, in case she misses the first time?" Josh is always so helpful.

"Shut up, you dorks. The first round's about to begin," I say. "And give me some of your fries. I don't know where my next meal is coming from."

The categories are kind to us tonight. Lots of sports. A round on twentieth century literature, which we ace courtesy of me, but which blows the other teams at Scotland Yard out of the water along with most of the North America leader board, except a team called The Borg. They're always there.

As we sit and drink our spoils, I tell them about my potential opportunity.

"Freelance. Remember that mortgage?" says Josh.

"Freelance. Wouldn't you be better off cleaning out your bank account to buy lottery tickets?" says Len.

"Freelance. Don't tell the bank. They'll recall your mortgage in a heartbeat," says Howard.

So nice to have friends that believe in me.

6

BDE's Canadian headquarters is downtown in an old building on Toronto Street. Simon's on the third floor, which is laid out in the typical rabbit warren of cubicles, some no bigger than a ledge attached to an acoustic panel. He has an office with a door but no window. It doesn't look like a very prosperous workplace and I guess my expression gives me away because once I've sat down on the guest chair, he says, "Most of us work from home a lot and we only bring customers into the boardroom downstairs, so there's no point in being fancy. We're all so busy, heads down, analyzing stuff, that nobody notices what it looks like. It's a heavy burden but very rewarding," he says. He pulls a three-inch binder from his shelf. "Easier to show than tell," he'd said, which is why I'm here.

"We did something similar to this project once before," Simon says as he detaches a bound 8.5-by-11-inch booklet from the binder. "I tell you, I learned everything I know about travelling from that other ROI study. It was brutal but worth it because now I'm a pro. And I scored about a million Marriott points. Anyhow, here's how it's going to work. We need to do fifty case studies spanning Europe and North America. The case studies will be the output from executive interviews where we find out about each company's ASP implementations and get them to quantify their benefits. It all has to be done within three months. I mean, not just the interviews, but the full report. That's why I need as many hands on deck as possible." As I'll later learn but was beginning to suspect, Simon is a master wielder of clichés.

Visions of swanning around Paris and Rome flit through my head, then go *poof* as he explains that Europe will be covered by the European analysts. Canada is also off the table because the Canadian analysts will be on the hook for that. What he needs me — or someone — to do is look after twenty-five of the case studies that will be done in the U.S. Or maybe not twenty-five, but up to twenty-five, depending on whether U.S. resources are available. "The thing is," Simon says, "everybody also has to do their regular day job, cranking out research reports and dealing with customer inquiries on the research. This kind of project is a big time sink because of all the hours spent on planes and driving rental cars to obscure places." Rental cars? Yikes.

Simon says he has the budget to pay twenty-five hundred per completed, customer-approved case study, plus all travel expenses. "That's in U.S. dollars, by the way," he says. He hands me the case study book and says I can take it home to peruse.

I take a deep breath and try my best to sound nonchalant. "Let me get back to you in a day or two," I say. "I need to check my schedule and availability. But thanks for the opportunity." He hasn't asked me a single question about what my qualifications might be. He must be desperate. But then again, I'm desperate too.

The book of case studies is two hundred pages long — single-spaced, I discover when I take a closer look at it. Each entry takes up four of the pages, including a full-page spreadsheet with costs and benefits projected out five years. There's a calculation for ROI percentage, another for how many years it would take for the software implementation to pay itself back, and another for net present value. This, I know how to do, courtesy of my MBA in finance. What a relief.

The write-up for each case study starts with a summary of statistics like the company's industry and revenue and a synopsis of the project. Then there's a background section. The first one I read, about a furniture company, says "A fable is told of an eastern monarch who challenged his wise men to invent a motto for his kingdom that would hold true in both good times and in bad. The one he selected, 'this, too shall pass away,' both comforts in times of despair and cautions in periods of prosperity." Hmmm. This is nothing like the boring writing I've done for consulting reports. Maybe this one is a bad example. I flip to an entry in the middle of the book, about a manufacturing company: "Shiny metal tools. Whirring machines. Fluorescent lights. Beyond the fear associated with a trip to the dentist, the average person probably doesn't give much thought to the devices and materials that might get embedded in his mouth." I move to the back section and find an entry for a candle company: "If you forgot to observe National Sense of Smell Day this year (it was April 28), perhaps now would be a good time to stop and smell the roses." Okay. This is a trend. And not one I'm happy to have discovered.

7

The HVAC sales guy is here to go over his quote. The line items span three pages. Single-spaced. He tells me the biggest challenge in houses like mine is where to put the duct work. Oh. I guess radiators don't use ducts. That had never occurred to me.

He walks me through the rooms, showing me where the work needs to be done. Basically everywhere. He rhymes off the tasks: create ductwork schematic, make channels in the ceiling and walls, remove the oil tanks, break up the boiler and get rid of it, take out the radiators. "For that," he says about the radiators, "you'll probably need to patch the floor afterwards. Or maybe replace it entirely depending on how good a job the guys do removing them. And you'll need to find a good plasterer. We open the walls but don't close them."

He goes on and on and on and on. Thermostats. Gas service installation. Refit the chimney flue. Replace the water heater. And, oh, did I want air-conditioning? Somehow, that wasn't in the original scope we talked about so it would be extra. We get down to the bottom of the list to a grand total of $10,999.99. The ninety-nine cents is a nice touch. Helps it pretend it's a friendly number, just like at the grocery store. Much, much, less than eleven thousand dollars. I tell him to leave it with me and I'll get back to them soon. "Don't delay too long," he says. "We're getting really backed up. Everybody needs this type of work done before fall."

I dare to do the math on Simon's proposition. Twenty-five hundred bucks times twenty-five equals sixty-two thousand, five hundred. American dollars. I go upstairs to press the modem into service and find the current exchange rate. 1.54798. So, in Canadian dollars that's $96,748.75. For three months' work. I could install almost ten furnaces and the spectre of my unsafe (according to my insurance company) knob and tube wiring still looms.

***

My friend Sue meets me for dinner at the greasy spoon Greek restaurant on the north side of Danforth at the top of my street. We grab a booth at the back, slide into benches with upholstery held together with duct tape, and wave down the waitress to bring a carafe of retsina. No need to look at the menu, they'll automatically bring us the usual: the chicken souvlaki special with extra tzatziki. "So," says Sue. "What did you think about the gig? Simon's pretty good to work with if you ignore his cryptic instructions and just do what you think he wants done. He'll change his mind anyway. At least three times a day."

I tell her I see pros and cons and I'm not yet sure which way to go. I show her the list I've made. The con side is pretty long. It's freelance, and I've never done freelance, and I'd need to figure out how to do billing and get a GST number to be able to collect tax and maybe incorporate, and doesn't it cost money to do that? There's no guarantee I'll get to do all twenty-five case studies and no guarantee they'll even pay me for work I've done because I might mess it up. I've looked at the case studies in the sample report Simon lent me. They are so insightful yet easy to read and the accompanying spreadsheets are a thing of beauty. How can I possibly deliver something like that? And also, being on the road for at least two months solid in another country.

Oh, and I'm almost forgetting the thing that should be at the very top of the list: rental cars.

"You know," Sue says, revealing the remnants of an English accent, "when my friend Sally and I packed up and moved to Canada it was on a total lark. We had no idea where we'd live or work. All we knew was Canada had the same queen. And that was good enough. It all worked out in the end. If we'd made a list of pros and cons, we'd still be answering phones and filing memos at the Rothmans cigarette factory." She lets me ponder this while she visits the loo.

When she gets back, I tell her the pro. There's only the one. Dollar signs. U.S. dollar signs. "That's BDE alright," Sue says. "Penny wise and pound foolish. Not that I mean he'd be foolish to hire you. Rumour has it that last ROI study was a shit show because nobody really knew how to quantify things that seem intangible. I've seen you do that with your hands tied behind your back, at insane client sites, on impossible deadlines."

"Yes," I say. "But did you ever hear me mention I liked that kind of stuff?" Plus, my inside voice says, it came with a regular paycheque and dental care.

Sue waves for the bill, looking deeply disappointed in me. She shakes her head and shrugs. "I can't push a rope, but how can you possibly have even the remotest notion of turning Simon down?" She's right. How can I? I need a furnace and to pay a not insubstantial mortgage and feed myself and the cat.

I channel my inner Sue and ask myself what's the worst that could happen, but at this point, I have no conception of what that would be.

8

Simon is giving me the full lowdown on the project in his office. This requires drawing things on his whiteboard. It appears that Sue was right. His attempts to simplify stuff seem to do absolutely the opposite. He's got a red marker in one hand and a green marker in the other hand and is creating what looks like a flow chart. It has arrows and swirls and things that double back on each other. He adds circled letters and numbers and then ends his diagram with a flourish at the bottom of the board: a funnel that collects all of the arrows emanating from the boxes scattered above. "So, there you have it," he says. "This is how our ROI multi-client is going to come together."

I try to look pensive instead of puzzled. I have a notebook open in front of me and a poised pen, but so far, the page is as blank as my stare. I need to find a way to make sense of this or I'll be in deep doo-doo and also, if I can't buy a new furnace, I'll be in a deep freeze come winter. I ask Simon to tell me all about his travels for the previous project. Maybe that will give me a clue about exactly what I'm going to be doing. Turns out Simon loves talking about doing the first ROI study. I've fired the starting pistol and he's away to the races, or actually away to the airport.

He reaches under his desk and pulls out a battered laptop case. It's made of scuffed brown leather and has a pocket on the front that's closed with a flap that turns out to be secured with Velcro and makes a ripping noise when he opens it. He takes out a passport and ruffles the pages. I can see it's littered with customs entry stamps. "This is my old one," he says. "It's completely full. I keep it because it reminds me how much ground I covered. Make sure your passport has lots of empty pages and hopefully you already know it has to be at least six months away from expiry. You are cutting it close to get a new one at this point." I cast my mind to the unkempt kitchen drawer that holds my dusty passport and try to remember when I renewed it last. Must have been a few years ago.

Simon keeps talking. "Have you seen those old suitcases in Goodwill with the stickers on them from exotic locations? My bag would look like that if it was one of those. Except for the exotic part. I've been to U.S. cities and towns I didn't even know existed and many I hope I never have to visit again." This does not sound particularly promising so far.

He goes on to tell me to plan on blocking off two or three or even four days for each interview, depending on how hard it is to get to. Apparently, the U.S. analysts will cherry-pick the low-hanging fruit like Chicago, San Francisco, and New York. Of course they will.

The interviews will all be booked for half a day, but it may not be possible to fly back right after the meeting. "Sometimes there's only one flight a day or there might be a four- or five-hour drive to get to the nearest airport," he says. "Also, I cannot stress enough the importance of conducting each interview in person. We learned that the hard way last time. It's too easy for them to blow you off if it's just a phone call. When you turn up at their doorstep, they kind of feel obligated to follow through. And always use MapQuest so you won't be late." Okay, so even if the interview is scheduled and confirmed it may not happen? How is that even possible? Did I hear him say 'four or five-hour drive'? And what's MapQuest?

The swirls at the top of his whiteboard diagram apparently represent the things we need to do first before we'll be ready to start interviewing. An interview guide, so the several people who will be completing the interviews will collect consistent information. A spreadsheet template for the ROI numbers. A set of ROI assumptions. A template for writing up the case study. A methodology for quantifying ASP benefits.

I would have thought they'd have all this stuff from the previous project, but then again, it didn't work out so well so I guess it's better to start from scratch. "If we screw up the methodology, we're sunk," Simon says. "Do you think you could take a stab at it? By Friday morning? Oh, and here's your contract. Can you get it back to me then too?" Today is Wednesday. Afternoon. Does the contract even cover this extra work?

"Sure thing," I say with my outside voice. My inside voice is calling me an idiot.

"But before that," he says, "I need you to meet your logistics team." He puts the phone on speaker and dials in to a conference line. Turns out I have a bit of a road crew. Robin, a travel agent in Toronto and Holly from the BDE head office near Boston, who will be recruiting interviewees and setting up my appointments. Robin will be booking all my flights, hotels, and rental cars. "I have an open requisition from BDE for travel bookings," Robin says. "You'll never see a charge. I assume you want only Marriott hotels like Simon. He's Platinum Elite already. Major perks. And just so you know, as a corporate travel agent, I don't work weekends. Or holidays," he says. This gives me an uneasy feeling, but I set it aside. It must work okay otherwise why would Simon use him?

Holly did all the recruiting for the previous project so knows the ropes. "You just need to tell me your schedule or actually it's easier if you just tell me when you're not available. I'll try to give you a week's notice before an appointment — that will help Robin too. I'll also try to group your meetings in the same general geographic area if I can, but that doesn't always work out. Remember when you had to get from Wichita to Hoboken in twenty-four hours, Simon? That was a nail-biter, but it was sure fun once we were finished," she says. I don't even know where Hoboken is and I'm a little dicey on whether Wichita is in Wisconsin or Iowa. Simon mimes bashing his head against the wall. Right. It felt good when it stopped.

"Um, Simon, this might be a dumb question, but I've never travelled a lot for business before. What do you usually wear?"

Simon looks a little baffled. "Wear? Never thought a lot about it. I just wear what everybody else does. My suit jacket. A pair of jeans. A polo shirt. I carry whatever else I need in a suit bag. I don't know what women wear. I never notice."

"One last thing." Simon hands me a piece of paper with the BDE logo and what looks like a business card. "Here's an important letter. Keep it with you at all times when you're on the road. And this is a calling card you can use when you're in the U.S. to phone long distance."

9

I rummage through my junk drawer for my passport. It's pretty pristine, aside from the detritus from the dusty drawer that sticks to the front. I peel off a decayed elastic band and a couple of mini Post-it notes. I can't remember the last time I cracked it open. The cover is so stiff I need to bend it forcibly to be able to see the expiry date page. Whew. It's good for another nine months. Next, I take a look at the contract Simon gave me. It's only one page with a one-page appendix with the terms and conditions.

Fortunately, it all seems in order. The price per case study is as promised and there is a provision for an hourly rate for other stuff. I'm assuming the methodology falls under that. It doesn't say I have to pay for travel costs up front, but I do have to submit expense reports. My daily meal allowance is a hundred and fifty dollars. Not bad. Maybe I can do what I did back in the day when I used to travel around Canada for Imperial Oil teaching people how to use Lotus 1-2-3 while being only one page ahead of them in the manual. I scammed as much free food from conference room lunches as I could and pocketed the per diem. Surely my meetings will include refreshments, plus don't they feed you on the plane? I mentally tally the extra big bucks I'll snag.

Now I need to get serious about the ROI methodology. I used to know this stuff when I was in business school but never had much use for it once I graduated. There are ten boxes up in my office full of artifacts from various jobs that I thought might be useful to some version of future me. I hope I have turned into that person. I couldn't bear to throw out my MBA assignments and notes. Too much literal sweat and tears went into them, not to mention that if I was to amortize my tuition and self-funded living costs, each page I cranked out would be worth about $2,000. Surely, I can get some return on that investment.

I climb the stairs to the third floor and assess the collection of bankers boxes piled up in the corner near the dormer window. Most of them have a list of contents, but the writing is either smudged or hidden by an adjacent box. I pull open the box on the top of the first pile and dump its contents on the attic linoleum. It's a bunch of file folders full of time sheets. I have no idea why I thought I would ever need these. I doubt there will be retroactive audit of billable hours by companies that have long since disappeared. I stuff them back in the box and use a black Magic Marker to write "garbage" on the top flap.

The second box in the pile feels a little heavier. I place it on its side and let the contents spill out. More file folders, plus a thick Cerlox-bound document. Once again, the folders only hold old time sheets. I leaf through them out of curiosity. Why would I have kept them? They show client names, project names, and hours billed. Useless. I turn over the document so I can see the cover. It says *Time and Expense Procedures Handbook*. This is another relic from the era when I spent several (non-billable) hours a week filling in time sheets to justify my existence.

I also don't know why I kept the procedure manual. If I ever work somewhere that requires time sheets again, they'll have their own bureaucratic take on how to make sure they wring every ounce of revenue-generating capability out of their employees. But just for fun and to revisit past trauma for no good reason, I open the book. There's a list of the usual professional services platitudes at the front: "our product is our people," "our services are second to none," "we have a bias for excellence." They forgot to mention, "we grind our employees to the nub," "you are only as good as your last billable hour," and "we can replace you at any time."

The second section explains the metrics we needed to meet and the rationale behind our billable quota. We had to log at least thirty-five hours against billing codes weekly. Why not 37.5? Because the firm was extremely benevolent and allowed some slack for administrative tasks, staff meetings (after hours, of course), and the occasional dentist appointment. "We stipulate that each consultant must log thirty-five fully productive hours each week. Remaining time can be billed to internal codes if necessary." The handbook goes on to say, "we expect two hundred and twenty billable days per year. This allows for weekends, statutory holidays, and two vacation weeks."

Wait. I'm guessing human resources will be a big part of the ASP's benefits. Why would a company want to outsource their software and computing power unless it was cheaper than retaining people internally? We'll need to know what their time is worth. I grab a notebook from my desk and start writing.

10

On Friday, I meet Simon at his office with my signed contract and a draft of the methodology. I ask him if I can use the whiteboard, which still holds his masterpiece. He picks up a marker, writes PLO in black, grabs some more markers and suggests we use the one in the meeting room." We walk down the hall and commandeer a small room with a round table and three chairs. "Everyone's always stealing chairs from this room," Simon says. "And they never clean the whiteboard. And the markers never work."

The whiteboard is really more of a greyboard, with many ghosts of previous brilliant discussions and the inevitable indelible remains of bad marker choices. Simon gives it a workout with the eraser without tangible results. He hands me the pens and tells me to go for it.

"Expenses will be the easy part of the methodology, so we'll talk about them last. The hard part is going to be the benefits," I say.

"You got that right," says Simon. "Took us months to figure out how to do that last time and we still didn't get it right."

Sure, Simon. Took you months and you still didn't figure it out and I'm supposed to pull it out of my butt in a day. "Anyhow, for the benefits we're going to need categories. I propose three: technology, people, and processes. That should cover everything they might save money on." Thank you, MBA strategy course! These components couldn't possibly have changed since 1985, could they? Simon nods. So far so good. "For technology, I think they'll either avoid cost by delaying or eliminating expected expenses, reduce cost by not having to pay as much out of pocket, and probably have something related to streamlining facilities costs."

"True," says Simon. "We already have a pretty good handle on the technology stuff and know how to ask the right questions for that. What else have you got?"

"People cost has got to be a big factor. Why would they do this if they aren't going to get some form of human resource benefit. Isn't payroll usually a company's biggest expense?" I say.

"Yes," says Simon. "But unless they are actually firing people, how can we quantify that? And probably any time saved is an hour here or an hour there."

Follow the bouncing ball, Simon. "What we do is ask them how much time gets saved, whether or not there is a real reduction in head count. Maybe they end up redeploying staff and don't have to add more. We can ask them what the average salary of an employee in a typical role is. We divide the salary number by 1,340 to get the cost per hour. Then just multiply by the hours saved. If we want to use full-time-equivalent bodies, we can divide them by 1,340." I set down my marker. Thank you, *Time and Expense Procedures Handbook*. QED.

"I don't get it," says Simon. "Where does the number come from? How are they going to buy into this?" Oh. I guess I bounced the ball out of the court.

I explain that the underlying assumptions are based on average working days per year and average hours worked per day. "We'll get the fully loaded employee cost from each company's HR department. They can't possibly dispute it. I think your clients will find our financial assumptions are very conservative. I mean, they'll think they are totally appropriate and sellable to their higher-ups. We'll still have to run all the assumptions by them, for this and the other categories of benefit, to get buy-in in advance. There's nothing worse that having them question a final deliverable."

"Yup, that's exactly what happened and it was the higher-ups that balked," Simon says. I tell him I'll package up all the assumptions so he can circulate them while we're busy building the spreadsheet. "We'll schedule a beta interview within the next two weeks," he says. "Fasten your seat belt. Might be a bumpy ride."

Back at home, I pull everything out of my knapsack onto the dining-room table to sort through the papers and notes I've collected so far. Best to keep my methodology working papers. I learned that the hard way when a consulting client disputed the amount of work we had actually done. Maybe that's why I'd kept the time sheets. Ass-covering habit. At the bottom of the pile, I find the letter Simon gave me. I forgot about the letter. It's addressed to U.S. border agents and says I work for BDE Canada and am paid in Canada and what I'm doing is conducting research in the U.S. that will be sold to Canadians.

I phone Simon. "Oh. Right. The letter," he says. "It's very important. Technically, because we are based in Canada, we aren't allowed to conduct business in the U.S. But the meaning of 'conduct business' has a little leeway. The most important thing is you cannot imply you are being paid out of the U.S. Of course you are, technically. But that's not important. The important thing is you don't want to get detained when you are crossing the border because that will grind this whole enterprise to a halt. But don't ever show the border guys the letter unless they ask. The first thing you do, if they ask why you're travelling to the U.S., is say you are going to a meeting or a conference. Only use the letter if they question you further. It might be a bit tricky because you'll be travelling at least once a week. Try and make sure you don't always go at the same time and for the love of God avoid being processed by the same agent two trips in a row."

11

I obsessed my way through the weekend trying to decide on a travel outfit. I landed on a more mainstream version of my telecom start-up uniform: a black silk sweater set, a beige pencil skirt, and, reluctantly, pantyhose. Instead of Birkenstocks, my feet are clad in the black pumps I bought when I turned forty, deciding they were something a grown-up ought to own. I have never worn them.

When I arrive at the airport early Monday morning, on my way to our try-it-out-and-see-how-well-it-works interview, there's a lineup that snakes the length of the long, squat terminal and doubles back on itself. The front part of the line disappears into a set of doors marked U.S. departures. Our flight to Atlanta leaves at eight thirty. It's seven o'clock. "Don't get there too early," Simon said. "I'll meet you at the gate." I decided to leave extra time, though, because of the whole border-crossing thing. The letter is safely in my laptop bag. I don't actually have my laptop with me, but I needed something to put my notebook and ID in, and I never carry a purse.

I join the end of the line, which is showing no sign of moving forward, but more people arrive behind me so I'm not at the end very long. I wonder what's going on. Surely it can't be like this every day. That would be ridiculous. Also, come to think of it, that would make my life a nightmare. I'm going to be here every week for many weeks to come.

The two guys in front of me are talking about their flights. "It's always like this on Mondays," one of them says. "You'd think Air Canada would have figured this out by now." Okay. Avoid Mondays then. But why did Simon tell me not to get here early? I guess he hasn't been on a Monday flight in a while. "We'll be okay," the other guy says. "Just wait and see. I think they'll have to pay us if they cause us to miss the flight. Too bad about my meetings though."

I stand still for half an hour, productively spending my time memorizing the pattern of the terrazzo floor. We start inching forward with no perceptible progress in the length of the line. Then I notice the people at the front part to let a uniformed airline employee through the door. "Anybody on the eight o'clock to Chicago?" she yells. The guys in front of me high-five each other, dash out of the line and get escorted to the inner sanctum. After they have disappeared, the airline employee comes out again and yells for passengers on the 8:10 to LaGuardia. A clutch of people heads to the departure doors. Next, it's the 8:15 to San Francisco. The 8:20 to Miami. The 8:25 to Boston. Aha. I see a pattern here. Sure enough, next is the 8:30 to Atlanta. My turn for a lineup reprieve. I follow the airline person to the visible front of the line and through the door. She bypasses the other fifty people who are already waiting in the inner room and leads me to a check-in desk. The agent opens my passport to the photo page, but barely looks up at my face, and hands me a boarding pass.

I go through a turnstile and walk down the corridor that leads to the customs and immigration hall. It's mostly empty. I hand my documents to the U.S. official, who also only looks at them briefly before handing them back. He doesn't ask me anything, not even where I'm going, but he could find that out from the boarding pass. No need for that letter today.

I find the gate and take a seat. No sign of Simon. I hope he shows up because I have no idea where we are going, once we get to Atlanta. But I'm here in plenty of time, at least thirty minutes before the flight is supposed to leave the gate. The lounge is starting to fill up but still no Simon. "Atlanta flight 832 is now ready for boarding," the scratchy PA system says. I decide to get on the plane. I turtle down the narrow aisle and find my seat. Miraculously, it's in the exit row. I'm pretty sure Robin would have booked us seats together, so Simon should be in one of the empty seats beside me.

I take the safety brochure out of the seat pocket and try to make sense of the pictographs. Interpreting pictures is not my strong suit. What I gather from the instructions for this Boeing 777 is there are many things I should not do in case of an emergency (the things with the big red 'X' through them) and some that I should, but I have no idea what they are. At least I know where two of the exits are.

After about twenty minutes of aisle shuffling, almost everybody seems to be on board and Simon is nowhere. Then just as the flight attendant announces departure is imminent, I see him saunter through the front door of the plane and make his way down to the seat beside me.

"Happy Monday," he says. "Wait, were you reading the safety card?" No point in denying it. I'm holding it in my hands. "The safety card is for amateurs. You gotta know, if this sucker goes down, we're dead. That's the deal."

"I was getting worried," I say. "Atlanta is a big place and I have no idea where we're going."

"I never miss flights. Missing flights is for amateurs," he says. "And Mondays are especially easy because there are so many people flying out. I know I'm going to get called out of the line, so I just show up at the last minute. Anyone who doesn't do that is an amateur." Good to know, Simon. Thanks for the info. And thanks for placing me firmly in the amateur bucket.

As the flight attendant begins her safety spiel, Simon unfurls *The Globe and Mail* and turns to the sports section.

Somehow, I thought we might spend the flight talking about our "proof of concept" interview. I guess everything will be revealed once we get there. Or at least, I hope it will.

***

The Atlanta airport is vast, but Simon makes a beeline to the rental car desk without even looking at the direction signs. His name is on one of those plastic boards where you can attach letters to spell out words. At the top of the sign, it says Budget Fastbreak. Simon heads through the glass doors to the parking lot and locates a spot marked H03. "Aha. My usual," he says, as he gets into a Buick LeSabre dad car. "I like lots of room. You have to sign up for Fastbreak as soon as possible," he says. "I'll drive this time, though." I'm guessing now's not a good time to tell him about the driving thing.

I slide into the passenger seat, snagging my pantyhose on the seat belt in the process. I watch as a stocking run gleefully races down my left leg and disappears into my shoe. I mentally subtract my hoarded per diem amount from my net take-home pay. I'll easily spend it on hosiery, if this is any indication of the half-life of in-transit legwear.

Simon hands me a page printed with a map and directions. "You can do the MapQuest thing," he says. So that's what MapQuest is. I'll have to check out the site when I get home. I read off the directions as we make our way to the interview. As a bonus, it eliminates the need for small talk. On the other hand, Simon still hasn't told me anything about how the interview is going to work.

Liberty Financial, the company we're here to see, looks like it's right in downtown Atlanta. In fact, all of Atlanta looks like it could be downtown because, near as I can tell, Atlanta consists of endless high-rise office buildings. Simon finds a place to park in the underground garage and we ride up the elevator to the eleventh floor. He tells the receptionist who we're there to see and we take seats on plush chairs in the waiting area. Finally, Simon takes a sheaf of papers out of his briefcase and waves it at me. "Right," he says. "I guess you don't have a micro tape recorder yet. Put that on your list too. We can use mine. Always bring extra batteries. Anyhow, I'll take the lead and you can take notes. Chime in whenever you want."

I don't tell Simon about my bad experience taping meetings. I did that once about ten years ago and swore I'd never do it again. For a ninety-minute meeting, there were fifty pages once it was transcribed. Every um and ah, and endless reams of small talk. Maybe things have improved since then, but I always find it better to take hard copy notes. Also, hard copy can never get accidently erased and a notebook can never malfunction — or so I thought at the time. I will learn later that's not completely true.

The receptionist ushers us into a small meeting room where our first ROI subject is waiting. He introduces himself as Donald, the CFO, and then asks us how he can help. I give Simon a questioning look, but he just launches into a spiel about the project and the importance of capturing information that will result in a robust analysis of return on investment. This seems to satisfy our interviewee, although I can't help but think he has no idea why we are here. Simon turns on the tape recorder.

"Let me tell you a bit about Liberty Financial," Donald says. "We are an integrated asset accumulation and management organization handling over $63 billion for investors through an array of annuity products, institutional accounts, and mutual funds." I scribble furiously, thankful that I have some grasp of the lingo, courtesy of my time spent in banking. Not happy time, mind you, but time nonetheless.

Simon starts his questions by more or less following the interview guide I helped prepare. He asks the CFO for more details about the company and what led them to decide to use an application service provider. Donald has lots to say and my pen continues its urgent journey across the page. Things are going swimmingly.

12

Until they don't. Simon goes way off the rails, letting Donald talk about all kinds of random stuff, like why he likes Atlanta (the Braves) and why he decided to become a CPA. I look at the clock on the wall. We have exactly one more hour to wrap this up and make our return flight to Toronto. Donald takes a pause and I jump in. "So," I say, "as a CFO you clearly have a handle on numbers. What would you say is the biggest benefit you've gotten out of your ASP implementation?"

"Well," says Donald. "I guess that would be the trophy right behind me on the credenza." He points to a gold-toned statue depicting what looks like a winged dolphin. "I won the accountant of the year award at the Atlanta chamber of commerce just a month ago." This is not going the way it's supposed to.

"Okay," I say. "Let's talk about the cost side of the equation. What kind of investment are we talking about here?"

Donald looks shocked. "You mean what we spent? I can't possibly discuss that. We are a private company." I feel like the cleat that's holding my rope to the sheer rock face has given way and I'm dangling fifty feet in the air. I transform my grimace into a smile and look over at Simon. I'm just the sidekick, after all.

Somehow, we keep Donald talking for another hour and I fill up most of a notebook. Simon tells him we'll draft the case study and send it to him in a few days. We take the elevator down to the parking garage. Simon looks at his watch and says we have ample time to get to our flight and maybe enough to grab a beer at the airport. He also says he's very pleased with our meeting. Lots of good stuff. My inside voice says we certainly got lots of stuff, but I don't think it will necessarily fall into the category of good. Or even remotely useable. Simon hands me his tape recorder and microcassettes. "You can use this to draft the case study," he says. Okay. I guess I'm drafting the case study by myself. Good to know.

We walk down the airport concourse, past a row of stores. "Oh. Hudson News," Simon says. "Let's duck in here for a minute. I need something to read." He examines a stack of self-help books displayed at the entrance. He picks up *Don't Sweat the Small Stuff* and reads the back copy. He points to *The Power of Now* and *Who Moved My Cheese?* and tells me he already has those. "Good books for business travel. Impresses your seatmate." I'm not sure why I'd be interested in impressing my seatmate, so I look at what else is on offer.

Fridge magnets! I could collect fridge magnets from everywhere I go. It'll be a travelogue decorating my fridge and I can start today. I select one in the shape of a peach with "Atlanta" written across the middle.

13

My laptop clunks and whirs as it comes to life. I have to get the Atlanta interview written up now or never. The cursor mocking me from the upper lefthand corner of a blank Word document thinks it will be never. Instead of putting fingers to keyboard, I liberate a highlighter pen from my writing implements mug. I've decided I should start by reading through my notes and marking the important bits. Surely there are some important bits.

Two hours later, I have notebook pages that show only sporadic swaths of Day-Glo yellow. Maybe the tape recording is a better way to go. I load the player with a microcassette exactly the size of one of those small boxes of wooden matches. The kind the guys in high school used to light using their front teeth. As the tape clicks in place and begins to play, I start to relive the disastrous interview. The readout on the front of the machine shows how long the recording is and where it is on that continuum: 00.05 of 245.08. I'm going to be listening for an extremely cringe-worthy while.

To my amazement, I discover there *is* some stuff I can use, especially if I quote Donald directly. I still don't know how we're going to get around his lack of disclosure of costs, but that can't be entirely my problem. Can it? I also think I can spin Donald's sidebar ramble into one of those intro vignettes like in the other ROI study. Something like, "The modern CPA is nothing like the old stereotype of rolled-up striped shirt sleeves and a green visor who commuted to work with a horse and buggy. These days, at forward-thinking companies like Liberty Financial, they embrace the computing workhorses at application service providers, and like Donald Boggs, earn the accolades of their peers." Brilliant! Simon's got to be impressed with my horse analogy. My fingers fly over the keyboard. I can type a hundred and twenty words a minute, thanks to taking typing instead of Latin in high school. Where are all those Latin scholars these days? Hunting and pecking with their index fingers. They may know how to say "revenge is a dish best served cold" as Caesar would have, but they have not lived it.

I log in to Hotmail, attach my draft case study to a new message, and just after I hit send, I get the ping of new mail coming in. Can't be Simon already. No, it's from Holly. *Interview booked*, the subject reads. I click it open. *You are going to Tacoma, Washington, in a week. Another financial company. Here's the address and details. Hopefully not as weird as the last one.*

Robin picks up after ten rings. "Sorry," he says. "Busy day today. Tacoma? Might be a bit of a problem. But never mind. Can you just email me the details and I'll send you the booking?" I forward him the email from Holly that says what day and time I'm supposed to be there. Once again, a problem that I'm sure isn't mine to fix.

But while I'm online, I might as well check out MapQuest. It is indeed an internet miracle. All I need to do is type in the address I'm leaving from and the address I'm going to, and voila, it supplies a map and written directions. Thank you, Simon. Finally, some useful information.

The phone rings when I log off. It's Simon, finally getting back to me about the Liberty Financial thing. Sort of. He says he won't be able to really get back to me for another week or so. His wife is doing the editing and she has to get an annual report done for her client. I tell him about the Tacoma thing. "I already know," he says. "Just go and do it. I think our interview guide is ironclad. We'll sort out Atlanta later."

When I hang up, the answering machine's light is flashing. This phone line has never had such a workout. *Robin here.* He explains that Seattle and Tacoma share an airport called Sea–Tac that's sort of between the two. Apparently if you go north up the Pacific coast, you get to Seattle and if you go south, you get to Tacoma. Who knew? He says he'll book me a car. And also, I can get there by the early afternoon because of the three-hour time change, but getting back will take all day. I'll need to stay two nights.

I ponder my reply. Should I tell him I lost my glasses and can't drive? My driver's licence expired and is in the mail? I have narcolepsy? None of those make me sound like I'm competent and trustworthy. I decide to take a different tack.

Robin's number rings and rings. I tell his machine I've never driven in the U.S. before (true!), I don't feel comfortable driving where I've never been before (true!), and I want to make sure I won't miss the meeting because it's really important (true!). I hang up quickly, in case he intercepts the call.

14

I have the full complement of gear in tow for this trip. I have a brand-new tape recorder, with extra tapes and extra batteries. I haven't yet tried it out, but I figure I'll have time to do that once I get to Seattle. I slipped the instruction manual into my laptop bag to read on the plane. I'm taking my laptop, hoping I can start the write-up for the interview on the trip home. It hasn't ever been carted around until now, just relaxed on my desk. Now it's time for it to show me its road trip chops. My Dell Inspiron 3800 fancies itself as sleek and light, with a fourteen-inch screen and weighing in at five pounds. I guess that counts as light. That's the weight of the wimpiest dumbbells at the gym, so it should be a piece of cake to carry it. Even though I'm not driving, I printed out the MapQuest instructions because after Atlanta, I discovered I don't like when I have no idea where I'm going nor how I might get there if worse came to worse.

Today, I've decided to wear a dress, which still requires pantyhose but it's just one piece instead of two or three. I've packed two other dresses and some extra shoes and am proud of how well I'm learning to travel light. I breeze through U.S. immigration once again, join the security line, and heft my stuff onto the conveyor belt. I walk through the metal detector and wait for my bags to appear. I finally see my carry-on but not my laptop bag. That's because the security guy has it.

He motions for me to step over to a table at the end of the rollers that ferry the bags out of the X-ray machine. "Miss, can you please boot this up?" he says. Hmmm. I don't remember if I charged it this morning. I wrestle the Dell out of the bag, lift the lid and press the power button. It lights up to show there's indeed battery juice. Hurdle number one. Then I wait, watching the pulsing green cursor on the upper left corner of the screen. And wait. And watch. After about five minutes, ghosts of the Windows 3 application icons start to appear, gradually gaining substance until they reach full form. I triumphantly turn the screen to the security guy and he nods and waves to dismiss me. A traffic jam of other laptop holders is restlessly piling up behind me, tapping their toes and checking their watches.

Crap. I forgot I was also going to have to shut this sucker down. I rummage in my bag for the mouse, spend another precious two minutes untangling the cord, and plug it into the port on the side of the laptop. I move the mouse to navigate up to the file menu. Nothing. Maybe it's because it won't work without the mouse pad. I rummage again and my hand emerges with a six-by-six-inch piece of dense foam that says IBM. So far, the Dell has not objected to this. I position the mouse on what I hope is its happy place and try to get the cursor arrow to go to the menu bar. Nope.

At home, I always just leave the mouse attached. Maybe it needs to be plugged in when the computer boots up in order to work. But I can't start it if I can't shut it down. Then I realize if I shut it down, my problem is solved. Time for drastic measures. I press and hold the power button. Five seconds. No response. Six seconds. No response. Seven seconds. No response. A serious amount of eye-rolling is evident in the crowd, and I fear the pitchforks are imminent. I persist because I have no other choice. Finally, after the longest fifteen seconds in the history of time, the screen goes dark.

I slap the lid closed and scurry off as quickly as I can, the Dell under one arm and its bag on top of the carry-on. When did they start making us boot up our laptops? How come Simon didn't tell me? Probably because only amateur travellers don't know. I'm not dumb enough to go through that humiliation again. One more notch in my travelling belt.

The chairs at the gate for the Seattle flight are only half full when I get there but I don't bother claiming one. I'll be sitting on the plane for six hours. I cram my laptop back into its case. There's a bunch of people sitting on the floor, banging on their keyboards. Maybe that will be me soon, although it can hardly be a very comfortable place to sit. That's when I notice there are power outlets about every ten feet along the wall, about a foot above the floor. Good to know.

"Attention Seattle passengers," a disembodied voice says over the intercom. "There will be an extra random security check for today's flight. If you are selected, please see the security personnel at the boarding gate." I hope this doesn't mean I have to reboot the Dell. It will likely not be happy about its forced slumber and decide to defy me by refusing to wake up.

The plane departure gets called and I join the line. As I search through my bag to find my boarding pass, I notice all the guys need to do is reach into the inside pocket of their suit jacket. Pockets. Why do none of my dresses have pockets?

I hand my boarding pass to the Air Canada employee and he types furiously into his terminal. He writes an "X" on it with a red Sharpie and hands it back to me. "Please see the pre-boarding security check," he says. Great.

I walk through the doors to the corridor that leads to the gate and see a security guard sitting behind a small table on a tiny chair that appears even smaller courtesy of his considerable girth. I hand him my Pass of Shame. He instructs me to place my suitcase on the table and open it. I unzip it and separate the halves and he immerses his rubber-gloved hands into my unmentionables to see what's underneath. My fellow passengers file past, then pause on the gangway right in front of the security table, waiting for a bottleneck to clear. On second thought, I would have much preferred to have to boot up the laptop again. I'm going to have to figure out how to bypass this. Either that or invest in much fancier underwear.

15

I've never been to Seattle before, but I guess I'm not technically in Seattle, just at the Sea–Tac Marriott. I get to cool my heels until tomorrow morning, when I go to the interview in Tacoma. The Marriott leans with full force into the whole northwest vibe. It's a sprawling two-storey building of the type that could only be situated in a locale where there's no shortage of land. The reception area is on the second floor and overlooks an atrium full of rainforest foliage and slightly creepy totem poles. I wonder if all Marriotts are this bizarre. There's also a meandering stream that ends at a pool that appears to be swimmable. I don't think I'll have time for that though. Simon told me it was best to keep myself on Eastern Time. "You won't be there long enough to get over the jet lag anyhow," he said. By my calculations, I should be in bed by seven thirty.

Simon was right. I'm tired at seven thirty so it isn't hard to fall asleep. I arrange for a wake-up call at six thirty, which will give me ample time to eat and get organized before the car service picks me up at nine.

My eyes snap open. Where was the wake-up call? I look over to the clock radio that's on a table on the other side of the bed. Its green digital numbers say 3:30. I'm wide awake. Of course I am. At home it's six thirty already. I turn on the bedside light and peer through the curtain. Pitch black. If I'm supposed to stay on Eastern Time, I guess I have to stay up.

I click on the television remote and flick through ten channels of static before reaching what appears to be an infomercial station. A woman wearing way too much makeup is whirring something in a blender. Maybe breakfast. She finishes her task and pours the bright green results into a bowl. Soup maybe? She picks up the bowl and takes it over to her left, where another woman is sitting in a beauty parlour chair. Hair dye maybe? But green? Next, she dons rubber gloves, dips her fingers in the green goop, and slathers it over the woman's face, all the while giving a running commentary on the benefits of parsley and cilantro for facial rejuvenation. I turn off the TV.

The manual for the tape recorder is lying on the bedside table. Might as well read it. Surprisingly, it has a lot to say about the teensy-weensy device. Ten pages of small print. The phone rings. I answer it, struggling to figure out who might be calling me. "This is your six-thirty wake-up call," it says. I guess the manual was less than scintillating. And now I've slept too much and ruined the time zone trick. Another check mark in my amateur column.

***

A black town car picks me up in front of the Marriott and heads south on Highway 5 toward Tacoma. I consult my MapQuest instructions and am glad to see my driver also seems to have MapQuest, because he's following the exact route I have in front of me. I can see the skyline of the city in the distance, on the other side of an insanely high bridge spanning some body of water. Even if I had convinced myself to drive, I couldn't possibly have driven on that bridge. As it is, I can barely passenger over it. I close my eyes and pretend to be napping and don't open them until I feel the car slow and then stop in front of the office building inhabited by Frank Russell Company. I tell the driver to pick me up in three hours.

I get out my notebook to double-check where I'm going, then take the elevator to the fifth floor. The mirrored door tells me my dress survived the plane journey admirably. My feet tell me that my kitten heel pumps are only marginally uncomfortable. I'm quickly learning I don't own the type of footwear that's up to the task of conveying me through endless airport corridors without causing my feet to complain, which I suspect is mostly because I'm not a guy.

Gene, the director of operations, is waiting for me in the lobby. Thank goodness. He clearly understands why I'm here. On the way to the conference room, he tells me Frank Russell is an investment firm founded in the 1930s. There are currently thirteen hundred people covering sales, research, and portfolio management.

"Our problem was the human resources system," he says. It was running on an ancient operating system and when Y2K was in the offing, we knew it wasn't worth our while to convert it." I can't believe how clear and concise this guy is. I ask him about costs and benefits and he pulls out a spreadsheet. He has his own spreadsheet already filled in!

"Can I get a copy of that?" I ask.

He hands me his copy. "Made this one just for you," he says. I try to read his watch upside down. Looks like I've only been here for an hour. There's got to be something else I need to ask.

"Are there any things you think make Frank Russell stand out as an organization?" I ask.

Gene thinks for a moment and says, "Have you heard about the falcons?" I tell him I have not. "So, every spring a couple of falcons nest on the 11th Street Bridge — the one you can see outside our window. We installed a camera on the bridge so anybody can watch them on the monitor in our lobby. The staff and customers love it!" he says. I write all this down. Then I truly cannot think of anything else I need, so I thank him and go down to the lobby. The only problem is my ride won't be here for another two hours.

I sit down on an upholstered chair, open my notebook and review my notes. Then I turn to a blank page and start writing the case study. No need to listen to the tape, it's all fresh in my mind. I'll have this done before I even get on the plane.

I've filled both sides of ten pages by the time my car arrives, right on time. Once we get back over the hateful bridge, the ride to the hotel is uneventful. I'm extremely pleased with my progress on the write-up. I'll need another hour or so to work on it, then I can go to bed early and have plenty of time to get up and pack before my six o'clock flight home in the morning.

But before I get down to work, I decide to change out of my work clothes into one of the more casual outfits I've brought. Maybe jeans and a t-shirt. Or my denim mini-skirt and a sleeveless blouse. Or the jumpsuit I added at the last minute, because I never know what I might feel like wearing. That's another weird thing I've noticed. Not many of the business guys I see at the airport bring carry-on luggage. At most, all they have is a suit bag. Just like Simon says he brings.

I finish typing up the draft of the case study. I'll still need to print it and make some revisions, but it's essentially done. I'll be able to watch movies on the way home. What could be better than getting paid to watch movies? Simon is going to love the colour I've added. "Frank Russell Company installed a 'falcon-cam' so employees and the local community can view the progress of the young birds on a TV monitor in the lobby of their headquarters. Moves such as this have given them a reputation as an exemplary employer, enabled by a high-end human resource system hosted by an ASP." A masterpiece.

16

"This is not at all what we want," Simon says as he hands me a document riddled with red pen marks. "I don't think we'll be able to use anything from the Atlanta meeting." I'm sitting in Simon's office. Dumbfounded. I know we didn't get any dollar amounts, but the case study part was pretty good. "Nancy said there's too much detail but not enough words. She said we need to reorganize things and take some stuff out. Can you do that by tomorrow?" Sure, Simon. With those clear instructions, no problem at all. I mutter something I hope comes across as noncommittal. Time to switch gears.

"Can we talk about the Frank Russell write-up?" I sent it to him last night.

"I only had time to glance at it," he says. "But what's with the falcon thing? How does that have anything to do with ASP costs and benefits?"

I've brought the book from the previous ROI project with me to give back to him. I open it to one of the case studies and point to the italicized paragraph at the beginning. The one that always has some folksy detail that makes the piece less boring, in my opinion. "I never thought including that stuff was a good idea. I don't think it's professional. At BDE we're studious and stick to our knitting. But Dennis overruled me. This time it's my ball game and I'm going to decide how it's played." Simon says.

I sit there for a moment, trying to figure out what to do. "Who exactly is going to read these case studies?" I finally say.

Simon looks puzzled. "I mean, who is the intended audience?" Something I probably should have already asked.

"Well, the sponsors will read them of course, but they are really aimed at prospective ASP customers," he says. Bingo. I tell him I was really impressed with how easy the case studies were to read. They were informative without being boring.

"I think the thing with ASP implementations is they'll tend to be pretty similar. It's outsourcing. How different can it possibly be? We're going to need a way to describe each company's experience so it isn't repetitive. Make it unique to them. I'm betting the only thing that will actually differentiate them is the nature of their business. And also, don't the subjects have to approve their case study? You know what Dale Carnegie said about a person's name being the most important word in any language." I hope I didn't lose him there. "Each company is going to want to be proud of how they are portrayed. That guy at Frank Russell was so excited about their falcons. I'm sure if we don't mention them, he'll be disappointed."

Simon says he'll see what Nancy has to say. "But what if the other companies don't have falcons?" he says.

I almost tell him we don't want the other companies to have falcons. That would defeat the purpose. But I think the better of it. I'll wait to see what Nancy has to say.

Back at home, I hunker down with the Atlanta write-up. It appears that Nancy doesn't like all the quotes from Donald. I guess that's what she means by too much detail. Maybe I can paraphrase them. That should make some words. I haven't had to pay so much attention to cranking out words since high school English class.

I sit at my desk until way past dark, cutting, pasting, moving stuff around. The Titanic's deck chairs now form a more pleasing configuration, in my opinion. Before I log off,

I check my email. Simon's name is at the top of the list with Atlanta in the subject line. At least I have a new version to send him. I click to open it to see what he has to say. Hopefully not more suggestions on what to change.

Forget about Atlanta. They refuse to let us publish any numbers and we can't have a case study with no numbers. Good thing it was just a trial run.

I close my laptop and rest my head on my desk. Twenty-five hundred bucks just vanished.

17

"Nancy says go with the falcons," Simon says on the phone, and I sense some reluctance in his voice. Or actually, more incredulity than reluctance. "I'm still concerned there might not be enough falcons. Make sure you always ask about falcons. We need to add that to the interview guide." At least we got that one settled, in as much as anything has been settled on this project so far. I'm not sure how I'll explain any lack of falcons moving forward, because I completely anticipate none will appear, but that's not a concern for today. There are a lot more worries where that came from. I'm pretty sure of it.

A call must have come through while I was on the phone, because the light's flashing when I hang up after my conversation with Simon.

Hi! It's Holly! Got you booked with some shoe company near L.A. They sound a little weird. Like, really secretive. Have a nice day!

Beep.

Robin here. Holly says Huntington Beach. A little hard to get to. Totally off the beaten path for a normal company headquarters. You'll definitely need a car. I definitely need to not need a car.

I invoke the powers of the internet and open MapQuest. I don't have an exact address, so I have to go with something approximate. L.A. airport to Huntington Beach. I phone Robin back.

After the usual ten rings, I get sent to voicemail. "Robin, I looked it up on MapQuest and Huntington Beach is only eight miles from the airport. Can you just book me a limo service?" I hang up and cross my fingers.

***

This time, I make sure my laptop is fully charged before I leave for the airport. Turns out nothing dire happened when I forced it into an unanticipated slumber on my trip to Seattle, so that's a relief. Today, as on every day I've been here so far, the U.S. border services agents all look the same to me: same buzzcut, same uniform, same surly expression. This makes it hard to follow Simon's advice to never talk to the same one each time. They are all the same one. But I'm counting on the fact that I'm still not an obvious regular, so I won't worry about that today. What I *am* worried about is the random security checks at the gate. I packed my best underwear, but still. Forget about airing dirty laundry, I object to airing clean laundry.

The security line is blissfully short. I'm sure I look like a pro as I boot up my laptop while waiting for my carry-on to appear through the X-ray tunnel. My case is doing this thing where it starts to appear, then gets sucked back into X-ray world. When it finally emerges, the security agent snatches it from the conveyor belt, places it on a table that's perpendicular to the conveyor and calls me over. "This your bag?" he asks. I nod to acknowledge that it is indeed my bag. "Open it, please," he says.

Seriously? I sigh and undo the perimeter zipper. He holds up the clear plastic cosmetic bag I use to hold my liquids and gels, which only consist of toothpaste, lip gloss, and one of those tiny bottles of moisturizer they give you in hotel rooms.

Oops. I forgot to put it in the tray separately. This counts as amateur, I'm guessing.

He asks me to take the toothpaste tube out. Rather than buy one of those small hundred millilitre ones, I've packed the dregs of a larger tube. A very clever move.

"Your tube can hold one hundred and eighty millilitres," he says. "That's not allowed."

"There can't be more than two squeezes left in there," I say.

"Your tube can hold one hundred and eighty millilitres," he repeats. He points to the garbage can that holds various other contraband and I dutifully dispose of it. I consider asking him how a toothpaste bomber was supposed to be able to fill a mostly empty tube with plastic explosive that he somehow managed to conceal somewhere in the departure area, but I think better of it. With the distraction of averting clear and present danger, he forgets to ask me to prove my computer is really a computer. Me: score one. Safety of the free world: extremely doubtful.

My new best practice is to be very observant at the airport. Not because of shoe bombers, but because being at the airport is kind of boring and watching what goes on can pass the time in a semi-amusing way. For example, one thing I've discovered is that planes going to a particular location tend to leave from the same gate or close vicinity. Like, for instance, the gate where the L.A. flight is going to leave from is across the concourse from the plane I took to Seattle last week. I'm not sure how or when this information will come in handy, if at all. Right now, it's just one of those observations that has insinuated itself into my brain and been filed in my virtual travel folder while I'm waiting in the departure lounge. Maybe that's what Simon meant when he told me he learned everything you could possibly know about being on the road during the last project. I'm already on my way to shedding my amateur status. No question.

As I suspected and dreaded, the staticky disembodied voice tells the lounge there will be random checks at the gate. I choose to hang back when my row is called to take a closer look at how exactly this plays out. I also notice a gaggle of other people — guys in suit jackets and jeans — that are not in a hurry to join the line. The first person in line gets "randomly" selected and I see the five people behind him get a free pass to walk through the glass doors toward the gangway. The sixth person in line gets "randomly" selected and I see the five guys behind him also get waved through the glass doors toward the gangway. Then the eleventh person in line gets "randomly" selected and again the five others behind him walk through the glass doors toward the gangway. This tells me all it takes to avoid being random is a bit of arithmetic.

I join the line and do a quick count of how many people are ahead of me. Looks like I'll be okay. I shuffle forward and sure enough, the woman in front of me gets pulled over. I hope she packed her best lingerie. I adjust my walking cadence to brisk and purposeful, in what I hope is a subtle way, but I don't fully exhale until I'm safely beyond the front door of the plane. On the plus side, I've learned yet another nugget to add to my roster of travel tips and tricks. At least until they change the rules again. As the saying about both horror movie plots and airline travel journeys goes, when you least expect it, expect it.

18

The L.A. destination Holly provided me with has a street name and number. Nothing else. I'm guessing this means the shoe company owns the whole building, but I have no idea what floor I'm going to and only the vaguest notion of who I'm going to meet. I have a hate–hate relationship with the unknown. I've invested every shred of my faith in a successful interview in the belief they will have an obvious (extremely well-appointed and dripping in infused organic fruit beverages) reception area staffed by Malibu Barbie. But despite my ridiculous Pollyanna tendencies, I'm getting a firm inkling this ROI gig is morphing into less of a seat-of-the-pants exercise and more into a question of whether or not pants were even involved in the first place.

A snappy-looking guy complete with peaked hat is holding a sign with my name on it in the baggage claim area. I identify myself and he says to follow him to the car. We take an escalator up two levels, cross a hallway, then take another escalator down three levels. He walks purposefully down a narrow corridor to what looks like a freight elevator and swipes a keycard on a device on the wall. At this point, I feel like I'm Agent 99 about to be delivered to CONTROL headquarters. I hope I won't be expected to know the secret password.

I'm relieved when we finally get to a parking lot full of Lincoln Town Cars. The driver opens the back door for me and rattles off the address I'm going to. I settle in to air-conditioned comfort as we roll almost silently toward Huntington Beach.

The car pulls up in front of a pink and yellow bungalow that's half a block from the water. The front yard has that kind of grass that looks like AstroTurf, or maybe it is AstroTurf, bisected by a worn flagstone path. This can't possibly be it. The driver shrugs and repeats the address he was given. I tell him to wait. I walk up to the door and ring the bell. I hear the sound reverberate inside but nothing else. I press the button again, holding it down for good measure. I hear some footsteps coming toward the front of the house and a person opens the door only as wide as the safety chain will allow. "Um, I'm here to interview someone from Skechers," I say. The door closes and I hear a muffled discussion between two people. The door opens again, this time without the safety chain, and a guy scans the perimeter of the front yard, paying particular attention to my black car. "He's with me," I say. "I'll just grab my stuff and he'll be on his way." This seems to satisfy him.

He remains standing in the doorway, and when I come back with my bags, he waves me inside. Although it looks like a residential building on the outside, the inside of the bungalow is done up as an office, with the living room acting as a reception area. The guy introduces himself as Brian, the vice-president of marketing. He looks like your typical surfer dude, wearing board shorts and a Hawaiian shirt with fluorescent pink flowers on a navy blue background. I'll be surprised if this company is actually a going concern. "I was expecting you," he says, "but we can't be too careful. Please sign this non-disclosure agreement." He hands me a five page, double-sided, legal-sized form.

I take a look through the document. I don't see anything alarming, but then again, I've never seen a non-disclosure agreement. I wish I could call Simon and ask him if it's okay, but that's impossible. Clearly this interview will not proceed if I don't sign. But if I promise not to disclose anything, how the heck am I going to write a case study? I decide that will be Simon's problem to sort out. I take the proffered pen and scribble my name on the appropriate line. "Can you make me a copy?" I ask.

Brian looks horrified. "I can't possibly let you keep a copy of our NDA," he says. "That would defeat the purpose." Well at least I can tell Simon I tried. I tell Brian not to worry. He looks relieved.

We head to what appears to have formerly been a bedroom, which turns out to be Brian's office. There are shelves on every wall surface that hold various styles of shoes. He gestures to a guest chair. I sit down and take my notebook and tape recorder out of my laptop bag. "No recording devices," Brian says. Why am I not surprised? This really *is* a spy caper. I stash my electronics back in the bag.

I tell him what I'm hoping to find out and he seems fine with it. I guess the NDA, or the "cone of silence," makes all things possible. I express my surprise at being deposited at a bungalow in suburban Huntington Beach instead of an office building.

Brian grins. "I know. Brilliant, isn't it?" he says. "Nobody would ever guess this is where we hatch all of our marketing strategy and campaigns. You can never be too careful in the athletic shoe business. A competitor can scoop something up and we could lose our shirts." I'm pretty sure losing his particular shirt would be a good thing, but I keep that thought to myself. I open my notebook and get prepared to learn everything I never wanted to know about sneakers.

19

Apparently, sneakers are a "thing." Brian tells me most basketball shoes never step foot on a court. "Our niche is 'lifestyle' footwear," he says. He goes on to tell me more about their business model. "We sell through third-party stores, that's our only bricks and mortar. We do most of our sales through our catalogue, and most recently, directly through our own online store." I get the store thing but not the catalogue or online. How do you buy shoes if you can't try them on? I ask Brian this exact question.

He looks at me with pity. "First," he says, "the limited-edition shoes are never meant to be worn so that's not a problem. Those sell out the minute they're announced. The other regular shoes are all in normal sizes. Everybody usually knows what size athletic shoe they wear. And really, they aren't meant to be used for things like running on a track. The only running people do with our shoes is errands. The teens wear them to school to impress their friends. That's about it."

Hmmm. These guys sell athletic shoes that aren't really athletic shoes. What's next? Gym clothes that aren't really for the gym? I'd like to see that happen! Or maybe I don't, given how most people at the gym look in their exercise outfits. Anyhow, Brian is still enlightening me on the world of selling to consumers online. E-tail, as he calls it, is the way of the future.

He explains that storefronts can only possibly keep a finite amount of stock on hand. "We have nine hundred different combinations of styles, colours, and sizes. No way can they keep all of that on their shelves. It would take a warehouse." And that's exactly what Skechers has, in a secret (of course!) location near the airport. The NDA continues to do its magic. It's like Brian is a Chatty Cathy doll with an endless pull-cord. Numbers and anecdotes and lessons learned and best practices spew out of him like a broken water main. This case study is going to be a real winner.

Two hours in, my hand is cramping from all the writing. I hope Brian doesn't confiscate my notebook on the way out. It looks like he's slowing down, though. He gets up and goes over to one of the fifty shelves rimming the walls of the room. "What size are you?" he asks. I tell him my ridiculously long and tragically narrow foot dimensions. He pauses only momentarily, then goes to consult the computer on his desk. "I can get you a Jenny in pink. New style coming out in two weeks. You'll be a trendsetter! If I ping the warehouse now, they'll have a pair here in fifteen minutes," he says. Nobody mentioned that taking swag from the interviewees wasn't allowed, and wouldn't it help in writing the case study to have a physical representation of the product to refer to? I decide the approach of asking forgiveness instead of permission is the way to go. I tell Brian I can certainly wait fifteen minutes because I still have to call the car service to pick me up.

***

I'm getting used to the hotels-at-the-airport approach. Gives me lots of time to work in my room and no need to get up early to make it to the flight. This Marriott even has a shuttle to and from the terminal and they gave me some toothpaste for free. Let me amend my previous statement. I'm getting used to hotels in general.

The hotel van lets me off in plenty of time for my flight home. I walk through the automatic glass doors, then bump my carry-on up a flight of eighteen stairs to the check-in area, because there's no sign of the escalators or elevators that greeted me on my arrival. The Skechers people probably manufactured the whole thing and just as easily made them disappear. True to California's brand and reputation (something Brian was very keen on), there's a group of bald, saffron-robed Hare Krishnas shaking tambourines and chanting, likely California granola crunchers who've embraced a life of devotion and poverty, which involves panhandling in front of fast food joints at the airport instead of working inside them.

My first stop, as always, is the Hudson News. The magnets on offer include tiny plastic licence plates, metallic palm trees, and miniature Hollywood signs. I pay for one of the tiny sign magnets and head to my gate.

***

It didn't feel right to try on my Jennys in front of Brian and I was too busy writing up the case study to do it at the hotel, so first on the agenda when I get home, after feeding the cat, is the Cinderella thing. The good news is they fit. The bad news is, with their aggressive neon pink colour and Velcro closing, my feet look like they're about to graduate from kindergarten. I guess sometimes you win at swag and sometimes you lose.

After a protracted internet search, I've discovered my falcon. "In his book *Little Dorrit*, Charles Dickens was the first to coin the phrase 'bricks and mortar' to describe high-street stores. Skechers is leaving old-fashioned notions of how to sell shoes behind, with their high-tech e-tail outlet, powered by an ASP." You've gotta love that one, Nancy. But I have yet to tell Simon about the NDA.

20

I attach my write-up from the California interview to an email and hit send. I decide to mention neither the NDA nor the free shoes to Simon until our regular status call this afternoon. In between now and then, I'll figure out what to say. Probably.

Meanwhile, my house is a disaster. There are holes in the walls from the HVAC guys and there's plaster dust everywhere. Even in places that defy logic, like inside the cutlery drawer. I'll only be home for two days until my next trip and no doubt there's more destruction to come, so I resolve not to waste my time doing any ambitious cleaning.

The cat's sitting on the kitchen couch, silently accusing me of deliberately tormenting him with the demolition mayhem. I moved the couch into the kitchen to get it out of the chaos in the living room, but it might stay here permanently, especially if the cat has anything to say about it. I refresh his water dish with a version that doesn't have a particulate raft on top, wipe his placemat, and open a new can of food. He sniffs at it, decides it's crap, and leaves a trail of plaster paw prints as he heads toward the back door.

I close the kitchen door. It swings both ways and has at least a one-inch gap between it and the floor, therefore it's unlikely to offer much of a barrier for anything airborne, but that's the best I can do right now. I grab a pad of bright pink sticky notes from the junk drawer and write *Please keep closed. And keep the cat inside the kitchen*, which I attach to the dining-room side of the door. I've cajoled the HVAC guys into feeding Ricky when I'm not home. Seems to be working so far and I'm paying them anyway, so why add cost of a sitter on top of that?

"So, Simon," I ask at the start of our phone meeting, "Is it normal for our interviewee to get us to sign an NDA? Skechers wouldn't let me in the door without it. I hope it's okay that I signed it." Best just to throw it out there. I prepare to duck.

"Some of them will want one," Simon says, "but we have a blanket NDA with all of our sponsors and that covers anything that might arise. They would only have nominated companies that are willing to talk to us." I guess Simon has forgotten about our trip to Atlanta. I refrain from reminding him. "Worst thing is we make them anonymous in the case study and don't mention a location." Really? I'm off the hook on that one? This emboldens me to fess up to taking the shoes. Worst case, I'll admit they are hideous and I would never wear them.

"Simon, if the company offers us some of their product, are we supposed to take it or politely decline?"

"If it's IBM and they offer you a free mainframe, I guess you'll have to say no," Simon says. "But only because how would you possibly get a mainframe on a plane?" He laughs, then continues. "Swag is perfectly fine. Product samples are perfectly fine, especially because they might help with your case study." Apparently, another bullet dodged. But wouldn't it have been nice to know these things before now? Yes, it definitely would. Note to self: try to remember to ask about things you don't know you don't know. Simon says, "I hear you're off to Atlanta and Augusta next. You're so lucky to get two so close together." Then he signs off without commenting on the beauty of my California falcon. *Que será, será,* or whatever the most appropriate West Coast saying would be. At least that one's from the movies.

True to form, my answering machine is blinking when I get off the phone.

Hi! It's Holly! You're going to The Salvation Army! Better be on your best behaviour or your afterlife may be a problem. This guy seems a little weird. Been in the service of God his whole life, as he was happy to tell me at length. I'd recommend not wearing a short skirt. You know what those religious guys are like.

Beep.

Robin here. Holly says Atlanta then Augusta. A little hard to do. Atlanta airport Marriott for sure, but then you'll have to take a short flight to Augusta after your Sally Ann thing. Itinerary on its way.

The good news is I don't have to change hotels. The other good news, as Simon said, is I can bang off two interviews in a row. No bad news I can think of.

***

I tell the cabbie I'm going to 1424 Northeast Expressway and the driver nods. I put my MapQuest page on the seat beside me and sit back. Just as promised by the directions, we circle around the airport terminal to exit toward the main highways. Then we merge onto I-75. This is definitely not what MapQuest says, but maybe he knows a different way.

Half an hour later, it doesn't look like we're anywhere close to my destination, even though my map says we should be there by now. But then again, maybe that doesn't account for traffic. I continue looking out the window for any sign of Salvation Army headquarters. After another twenty minutes, I rap on the plexiglass between me and the front seat. "Shouldn't we be there by now?" The driver shrugs. "But my directions say we should have been there twenty-five minutes ago."

"You have directions?" the driver says. "Why didn't you tell me!" Um, because you're the cab driver and I'm from out of town? He takes the next exit and pulls over to the curb. I hand him my MapQuest printout and he studies it for several minutes. "Aha! Northeast Expressway. Did you tell me Northeast Expressway? We have to go back the other way." Good thing I have a healthy time buffer. And an equally healthy credit card limit. I could probably have taken a helicopter for what this is going to cost.

The Salvation Army headquarters for the southeastern United States is located in a squat brown building near an industrial park. I don't know much about the Salvation Army other than brass bands on the corners at Christmas and thrift stores. They take the "army" thing seriously, though. Lieutenant Colonel Marvin Mosley (call me Marvin), the CFO for Southern Territory, is decked out in full regalia: a blue suit with epaulettes on the shoulders, and on each side of the jacket collar, six-sided red patches with a white "S" in the middle.

The lieutenant colonel shows me into an enormous office with wood wainscotting, plush green carpeting, portraits of lieutenant colonels past, leather-bound books trimmed in gilt, a chandelier, a desk the size of a Buick, and inexplicably, an array of silver candelabras on the credenza. I can't help but think about the board game *Clue*: the colonel, in the library, with the candlestick. I'm pretty sure I'm not in mortal danger, but if I am, I don't think Holly would be surprised.

I'm here to learn about the Sally Ann's new accounting system. Marvin says a recent change in the generally accepted accounting principles (GAAP, as accountants refer to them) caused a big headache. He is clearly as passionate about accounting as he is about feeding the poor and housing the homeless. Maybe more so. He retrieves a book from a massive shelf behind his desk. "This is the GAAP update from last year," he explains, as he describes in excruciating detail what the changes entailed. "We have four hundred centres of operations in our territory," he says. "I'm talking everything from daycares to uniform stores. Used to be each one could handle their own accounting needs and we didn't need to do anything but collect year-end statements. Now, everything has to roll up to the division level. I'm sure you understand the implications of that." I don't, actually, but best not to give him enough-rope-to-strangle-me-with details.

On the other hand, I'm discovering one thing that's good about dealing with an accountant: he has all the costs and benefits already calculated, complete with assumptions and footnotes on how they were derived. My job is thankfully reduced to getting the history of the project, the challenges and the outcome, all qualitative stuff I can fluff up to make more readable. I'm not sure I even need a falcon. Isn't the folksiness of the Sally Ann falcon enough?

21

As the Lieutenant Colonel and I wrap up the interview, a woman bustles into his office. Marvin introduces her as his wife, Manuela. "Manuela here has been by my side throughout my career," he says. "I met her in Miami when I was posted down there. She'd just arrived from Cuba." Manuela insists I stay for lunch and far be it from me to object to a free meal. My expense account will thank me.

I take a bathroom break and am a little disappointed they don't have branded toilet paper — that would be swag worth having — then I join Marvin and some of the office staff in the board room. As we chit-chat before the food arrives, Marvin compliments me on how good my English is and asks how much snow we have back in Canada. In June. I'm saved from a response when Manuela comes in with a bunch of sandwiches and what looks like packets of potato chips.

"I have a special treat," she says. "Cubano sandwiches! Marvin got addicted to these when we were living in Miami."

I have no idea what a Cubano is, but it's on a good-looking bun, I'll give it that. I take one from the platter in the middle of the table and grab some chips. I can tell the sandwich has some kind of cheese. Cheese I can do. I am the pickiest eater known to man, or at least known to my mother, who was a dietician. She was constantly forecasting my immediate demise from malnutrition (spoiler-alert, it has not happened so far) when she was in control of what was on my meal plates.

I sneak a peek at the sandwich innards. There's a slice of ham and some mystery meat. And mustard. I do not have a problem with mustard, but I do have a problem with meat. I don't have an ideological problem with meat, I just don't like it. Like, seriously don't like it. Like, we're talking barfing, and I do not want to barf in front of the fine folks at the Salvation Army Southern District headquarters.

Meanwhile, Manuela is waxing eloquent about her love of Cubanos and how hard it is to get a good one in Atlanta. I attempt to divert her attention from my lack of Cubano enjoyment by opening my chips. I have to appear to be eating something. I pop a few in my mouth.

These do not taste like potatoes. They taste like something very weird. I look at the package more closely. Plantain chips. I try not to panic. I'm allergic to bananas. You know, the innocuous thing you feed to babies once they're ready for solid food. Apparently, I used to spit them out onto my high chair table. I see this as a sign of my instinct for self-preservation. My mother saw it as a sign of my lack of desire to conform. I think we were both right. Nothing life-threatening has happened so far, just hives, and once when I unwittingly drank banana liqueur (unadvisable on many levels), my entire face swelled up.

However, I'm banana-savvy enough to know that both they and plantains are in the Musaceae family. They are kissing cousins and therefore shouldn't be anywhere near my mouth. As surreptitiously as I can, I spit the chips into my napkin. I wait a beat, then stand up. "I'm so sorry, I didn't realize the time. I have another appointment. Thanks so much for lunch. I'll take this to go! We'll be back in touch once the case study is ready for review," I say while I gather my things and make good my escape. I hope I didn't ingest enough plantain to make this trip disastrous.

When I get out the door, I look to see if there's anywhere I can ditch my sandwich and toxic chips. There's a dumpster a few yards away but I can't see an obvious opening into which to fling my uneaten lunch. As I'm contemplating disposal options, Manuela comes out with a Virginia Slim in her mouth, flicking a BIC lighter, walking purposely toward an area to the left of the building that appears to be a refuge for smokers. She seems too intent on her nicotine mission to notice me, but just in case, I make a show of purposefully stowing my sandwich in my laptop bag, then make a beeline to the corner where my driver is waiting to pick me up.

I hop in the back seat. "Back to the Marriott," I say. I settle in and open my bag to get out my notebook and review the results of the meeting.

"Hey," the driver says. "Is that a Cubano I smell? Haven't had a decent one in years. Where did you get it from?"

It occurs to me this is an ideal opportunity. "Want it?" I say, "It's untouched." I lob it over to the front passenger seat. "Plantain chips, too. Just as long as you don't eat them until you've dropped me off." Disposal mission accomplished.

22

The flight to Augusta is one of those typical business commuter things. It will take just under an hour and I'll be back in Atlanta in time for dinner. It's a Bombardier Dash 8, a small plane that holds thirty people, with two seats on either side of an aisle not nearly wide enough to accommodate a food and drink trolley. I get two seats to myself, either because of Robin's magic or the relative popularity of flying to Augusta on a Wednesday morning. There'll be barely time to ascend before we start to descend. My peach yogurt from the grab-and-go in the hotel lobby will have to tide me over until my next meal presents itself. It didn't taste like it had a passing acquaintance with a peach, even though Georgia claims to be the place where peaches were invented.

After several travel outfit trials and errors (mostly errors), on this trip I'm wearing a suit because I've learned that having pockets is essential. I can't imagine how I'd pull off the guys' polo shirt, jeans, and suit jacket combo without looking ridiculous, so I've stuck with the matching pants, which also dispenses with the pantyhose. I've already ruined ten pairs. I've stashed two blouses and some gym clothes in my carry-on, with ample room to spare. Maybe the guys are onto something with those suit bags.

Outside the plane window the weather looks just fine. Clear. Not yet hot and hazy. I'm kind of liking Atlanta and looking forward to seeing Augusta. At the very least, I'll pick up another fridge magnet. I settle into my seat, going through my (by now) typical routine. Put on a cardigan because planes are always cold. Place my reading material in the seat pocket. I may not read anything, but good to have it close at hand. Slide my laptop bag horizontally under the seat in front of me, handle facing forward for easy access.

The taxi to the runway is so long it feels like we've driven halfway to Augusta. Robin says Atlanta's the busiest airport in the world. I have no idea why. It would seem to me that New York or Chicago or Los Angeles should be busier. But that's just in the U.S. What about London or Paris or Bombay? But nope. Atlanta gets the crown.

After the seat belt sign is turned off, the flight attendant comes down the aisle, passing out bottles of water she's juggling under both arms. I've been writing the Salvation Army case study in my head, although I really should record my brilliant thoughts more permanently because I know I'll never conjure them up again. I take my laptop bag out from under the seat and retrieve my notebook. I lower the seatback tray, put pen to paper, and scribble away.

We seem to be going through some turbulence, which is making my normally bad handwriting look like a seismic wave, but I'm kind of used to turbulence now. Apparently, it's unlikely that the plane will fall from cruising altitude. But unlikely doesn't mean never. I recheck the snugness of my seat belt and continue documenting my meeting with Marvin.

The turbulence has abated, and the flight attendant has loaded herself up with more bottles of water, continuing her hydration mission. This time she looks a little concerned. Have we not been drinking our water? Is she running out of bottles?

Then the pilot makes an announcement. "I have to report a tiny issue," he says. "My gauges tell me there's something wrong with the engine. I'm not sure what, but to be on the safe side, we need to turn around and go back to Atlanta. Please stow all your items and make sure your seat belts are securely fastened. I know Carrie just gave you all water, but she's going to collect it again. Sorry for the inconvenience. Better to be safe than sorry. Please consult the brochure in your seat pocket for the procedures for a crash landing. Thank you for flying Southwest and have a nice day."

What did he just say? Oh, wait a minute. Something about crashing. But also, something about having a nice day. Which is it? I latch my tray, put my notebook back in my laptop bag and restow it under the seat. Nothing to do but sit and wait.

Except my brain does not agree. It apparently has lots of things to do. Who will look after the cat when I die in a plane crash? Who'll collect my bag from the hotel room? Can Simon kill me for not delivering my interview notes if I'm already dead? Wouldn't it have made more sense to continue to Augusta rather than spend more time returning to Atlanta? Should I be asking for danger pay? And what exactly is the statistical probability of dying in a plane crash? I do not know the answers to any of these questions.

It seems to take several hours for the plane to make a huge U-turn to reposition ourselves toward Atlanta, but it can't be more than fifteen minutes. The flight back is sombre, with side notes of panic, especially on the part of the flight attendant who is sitting in a jump seat facing us with eyes as wide as missing manhole covers, looking like she's not-so-silently repeating some prayer or other.

My brain continues to indulge itself. Does the engine sound like it's struggling to keep us in the air or is that just my imagination? Is that diesel fuel I smell? Why do I see the flaps on the wings moving up and down? Why is the pilot so silent?

23

Twenty-five minutes later, which by my calculation means we were five minutes away from Augusta when we doubled back, we land at ATL. When I look out the window, I see we're somewhere on the far reaches of the airfield on a slab of tarmac that's eons away from a gate.

I can hear sirens approaching and see a phalanx of fire trucks and ambulances pull up to the plane, but as far as I know, I'm not dead. At least not yet. I see the firemen unfurl a giant hose and, based on the liquid that starts pelting against the windows, spray the plane with full force.

There's a protracted period of radio silence, while I'm assuming the EMS crew is communicating with the pilot and maybe with the nearest funeral home. Finally, there's an announcement. "The fire retardant's just a precaution, folks. We're going to get the maintenance crew to check us out. We'll be moving to a gate to make that happen. Thanks for your patience. We hope to be back on our way to Augusta in about two hours." Two hours? I'm definitely going to miss my meeting. Not to mention, why would I even think about going there on this plane?

The ambulances are departing, sans occupants, which I take as a good sign. The plane starts to slowly taxi toward the terminal. Way, way off in the distance. We bump along for about half an hour until we finally reach a gate. Or almost reach a gate, because we stop short of it. "Folks, they weren't expecting us to need a gate," the pilot says. I'm sure he didn't mean for that to sound like it sounds. "We'll have to wait here for a bit."

I flag down the flight attendant, who looks only slightly less agitated now that we're on terra firma. I ask her if I can possibly get off the plane once we're attached to the gate. "I don't think that's allowed," she says. "We can't be responsible for people who don't take the flight. You'll still have to pay." Right. What about the part of maybe being killed in a plane crash on the way back to Augusta? Would you not be responsible for that? But I get it. If I was dead, I wouldn't be able to complain. Or sue. I sit back down and regroup.

We stay stuck on the plane for an hour. This gets my crisp-suited fellow passengers riled up enough to start loudly expressing their displeasure, which maybe prompts the pilot to finally make another audio appearance. Pilot speak is another thing I'm learning. Maybe they teach them that in pilot school. "Anyone who no longer wants to continue to Augusta is free to leave the plane once we get an external stairway situated. Should be soon. As you know, there will be no refunds for your flight, but thank you for flying Southwest. Have a nice day in Atlanta or wherever your travels take you." Clearly, not to Augusta.

When I finally reach the airport concourse, I'm relieved to see there's a bank of payphones on the wall adjacent to the bathrooms. I'm also relieved to see a bathroom, but in a panic, before visiting the facilities, I rifle through my notebook to find the number for Greater Augusta AutoParts and get out my calling card. I probably should have examined it before now. Looks like what I need to do is dial an eight-hundred number. I dutifully enter the digits on the card. "Please enter your access code," the robot operator says. I turn the card over. It's blank. Did Simon give me an access code? No time to puzzle that one out. I fish out some quarters out of my wallet, hoping Canadian coins will work. Low and behold they do. Yet another piece of information that would have been nice to know in advance.

I'm sweating and apologetic as I explain about the plane and the impossibility of my making the meeting. "Wow! What a thing! Hey, why don't you just phone me when you get back to your hotel room? No reason we can't do this by phone," the client says. No reason not by phone. Hear that, Simon?

The call takes slightly more than an hour. Less time than it took to not get to Augusta. It turns out, the hardest part of being in the auto parts business is keeping track of all the parts. The guy at Greater Augusta AutoParts uses an ASP to host his inventory management software. Lost parts cost money and not being able to locate a part results in a lost sale. It couldn't possibly be more straightforward. I'm not sure whether I'll tell Simon about the aborted flight to Augusta. Maybe it would garner some sympathy. On second thought, it's more likely to garner Simon's stories of near-death experiences on planes. He doesn't need to know it was a phone interview either. Or maybe I will tell him it was over the phone, but say the interviewee insisted or the meeting would never have happened. That's the truth, after all.

***

In my new routine, my answering machine is my first stop when I get home. It does not disappoint.

Hi! It's Holly! You're going to San Francisco. It's a magazine this time. Sounds a little weird. It was murder to get a live person on the phone. Only a machine. No receptionist. Robin's on the case.

Beep.

Robin here. Holly says San Francisco. It's a little difficult to get a flight on short notice. Very busy during the week. I'll let you know what I come up with.

24

The *Business 2.0* office is right near the San Francisco airport in a business park. Business parks, of course, exhibit absolutely no parklike characteristics. In the manner of all airports, SFO is nowhere near the city centre or other highlights of the Bay Area. I am getting to be an expert at being somewhere I'm not really at.

Everything is "2.0" these days. This fad started when the perils promised by Y2K fizzled like dud fireworks as we partied like it was 1999. Or, actually, didn't really party because most of the people at the New Year's Eve dinner I attended were on call in case planes started falling out of the sky or automated teller machines stopped working. Since they had already accomplished everything deemed doable to prevent this, I'm not exactly sure what was going to happen if they were called in. But of course, none of that came to pass.

The 2.0 stuff is supposed to represent a renewed spirit of innovation, courtesy of a new century. *Business 2.0* is a magazine, this much I know. The background information I've been able to gather says it was started in 1998 to publish articles about e-commerce businesses and their market niches.

The office building has a gold-coloured mirrored exterior, a style popular in the exuberance of the early 1990s that will forever reveal its provenance loudly and clearly. *Business 2.0*'s home is on the second floor, which is accessed via an open staircase leading up from a zombie foyer that lists the names of the tenants and their suite numbers. No concierge, no sign-in, no security whatsoever. On the other hand, I guess there's not much you can steal from a magazine.

The wooden door to suite 202 is closed, but the handle turns easily. It opens to a small reception area with a desk but no guest chairs. There's a bell on top of the desk and a sign that says, "Please Ring." I do as it bids, looking at the art on the walls as I wait. It's framed covers of every issue of the magazine, including the first one, June 1998, which featured eBay as the cover story. It also shows a retail price of $10.00. The only thing I know about magazine prices is what I pay for the ridiculous number of them I buy each month. The most expensive one, *Vanity Fair*, costs $2.75. I guess *Business 2.0* is a licence to print money. I ring the bell a second time.

This returns some results, as a guy dressed in casual Friday attire, even though it's Tuesday, saunters into the room with headphones looped around his neck. "You from that ASP thing?" he asks. I answer affirmatively. "Sorry, I didn't hear you at first. I was listening to my tunes. Come on back into the place where all the magic happens," he says. He tells me his name is Alan and that he's the publisher.

We enter an open-plan space that's scattered with desks sporting surfaces in various stages of clutter consisting mostly of piles of computer printouts. A coffee station in the corner burbles away. Other than that, it's completely empty of humans, except for my host. Maybe he runs a lean shop or maybe he uses lots of freelancers who work from home.

"We might as well use the boardroom," Alan says, as he leads me to a glass-enclosed room by the windows that's reminiscent of a gigantic display case. Even the table is made of glass. Oddly, there's a sleeping bag on top of an air mattress in the corner. Alan doesn't seem surprised by this.

I grab one of the Aeron office chairs (which are thankfully not made of glass) and carefully place my note-taking equipment on the table so as not to mar it. While I'm getting myself organized, Alan's rolling up the sleeping bag and deflating the air mattress. "I crash here sometimes," he says. "I live in San Jose and it's a bit of a commute on the 101. We could have had an office there, but I wanted to make sure we had a San Francisco address. It's a lot more expensive but has much more street cred. That song really spoiled San Jose for all of us. Makes it sound like a sleepy suburb." I guess he's talking about "Do You Know the Way to San Jose?" I wouldn't think that song was relevant to anyone's current opinion of San Jose since it came out in 1968, which is also clearly long before he was born. But what do I know? I've never been to San Jose. Nor the real San Francisco, for that matter.

We launch into the interview. I'm getting really good at this. I hardly need to consult the question guide anymore. Alan tells me profit at the magazine took a big hit in the last quarter of 2000. "Before the bubble burst, we were rolling in advertising revenue," he says. "Now we've gone from being a monthly to a quarterly to cut costs." Aha, that kind of explains the sparseness of office inhabitants. "But now we're on a different track. We've started an online version of the publication. Now we're truly in 2.0 territory."

I'm having a little trouble getting my head around this. Not the notion of moving online, but the notion that a publication aimed at e-business wasn't online in the first place. But what do I know? Surely, they must have had a good reason.

Alan continues his monologue. I guess he doesn't get to talk to many live humans in the course of an average day. He tells me the hard part is getting print advertisers to pony up for online ads. "When you have a hard copy magazine," he says, "it lies around for a long time and readers are exposed to ads over and over again. It usually passes through many hands as well. Turns out people find online ads annoying, all that popping up and stuff. We had no idea!"

Once again, I'm flummoxed. It appears that an enterprise that's built around advising online businesses has no idea how to become a successful online business. But what do I know? Surely, they must have a good handle on their business model.

I diligently continue to collect all the content I need for the case study. I wrap up by telling Alan he'll get a draft for review in about three weeks. "Any chance we can get it sooner?" he asks. I tell him I'll do what I can, thinking maybe I can convince Simon to speed it up. After all, the sooner the client approves the draft, the sooner I get paid.

I gather my stuff and make my way back to the entryway, where a mailman is unloading envelops on top of the unmanned desk. I notice most of them have red letters on the front that say "Past Due." This does not fill me with that blissed out feeling that's supposed to come with being in San Francisco.

25

It's stinking hot when I get back home from California, but the good news is the HVAC guys seem to be finished. There's a fancy electronic thermostat on the wall in the dining room and an instruction brochure on the table. I pick up the booklet and leaf through it. Seems fairly straightforward: hit the "On" button, select air-conditioning, and set the temperature. I do exactly that.

I'm impressed with how silent the system is. It makes me glad I chose the fancier model instead of cheaping out. "It may not be the most exciting way to spend your money," the HVAC guy said, "but you'll never regret buying the best equipment." I go into the kitchen and open the fridge. There are a couple of unopened single-serve yogurt containers with a best-before date of sometime last month. There's some sour cream that also says I should have finished using it up long before now. How do you tell when sour cream's gone off? But the milk is definitely off. Other than condiments I thought were a good idea at the time — red pepper pesto, bacon marmalade, rhubarb chutney — that's all there is.

I take a notepad out of the junk drawer and several pens. The fourth one I try works. I put the others back in the drawer, then take them out again, throw them in the garbage, and start making a grocery list. As I'm doing this, I notice it's still pretty warm in the house. I put my hand over the shiny new register in the floor in front of the window. Nothing.

I go back into the dining room and look at the thermostat. It still shows the information I entered when I asked it to please cool the air down to twenty-two degrees Celsius. I decide the best thing to do is implement the usual solution for electronics that are misbehaving: reboot. I hold the "Off" button down for the five seconds recommended by the instructions, plus five more *Mississippis* for good measure, wait for the thermostat to come back to life, and re-enter the coordinates that are supposed to result in air-conditioning. Nothing.

Now I'm a little miffed. Okay, maybe more than a little miffed. Because it appears I just dropped several thousand dollars on air-conditioning that doesn't work. It's after five, so it's doubtful anyone will answer, but I call the HVAC company anyhow. The voice on the answering machine listens passively to my problem for about a minute, then cuts me off in mid-sentence.

I'm relieved when the HVAC crew shows up at nine o'clock the next morning. I explain again what happened, or more correctly, what didn't happen. As they get to work, I take my newspaper into the kitchen to catch up on what's happened north of the border while I was away. I've started to notice that U.S. news has very little to say about anything that happens outside of the country. Even the TV weather map has a void above the U.S. border. Canadian weather literally drops off the map, despite the fact that in the winter they're quick to blame snowstorms on us.

I finish the front part of *The Globe and Mail* then move on to the business section. There's still a litany of tech companies going under, but one article in particular catches my eye. And catches my throat. According to a Reuters report, *Business 2.0* has gone under. It even quotes Alan, the publisher. "Our venture was a bold, innovative foray into the new world of business. We were clearly too far ahead of the curve." Sure, Alan. Sounded to me like instead of being bleeding edge, they were shedding blood in a different way, by hemorrhaging money. I wonder if Simon knows.

I hear a knock on the kitchen window. An HVAC guy. I open the back door and see that he's been messing with the AC unit that's attached to the back wall of the house. "I can't figure it out," he says. "Maybe this one is a dud, for some reason. I think we'll have to replace it. The good news is it's under warranty. The bad news is we won't be able to get to it until next Wednesday. With all this heat, everybody's clamouring to get their AC replaced."

26

The HVAC guys have returned with a new AC unit. It takes the better part of the day to replace the old one and I'm certainly not going to let them leave until they prove it works. The head guy fiddles with the thermostat while I hover over the register in the dining room. He punches a few buttons, thumbs through the manual, then punches more buttons. Still no cold air. He goes back outside to do something, comes back in, and punches more buttons. No cold air in evidence. He asks to use my phone, and I show him to the cordless set in the kitchen.

I wait with a distinct lack of cool heels, while he consults with somebody I hope is an air-conditioning whisperer. After about ten minutes of conversation, he hangs up and comes back into the dining room. "Nobody seems to know what it is. I guess we'll order another AC unit," he says. I tell him to do whatever they need to do to fix it and show him to the door. Based on the gust of air from the front porch, it seems ten degrees hotter in the house than outside. At this rate, I'll get working air-conditioning in time for Christmas.

Opening windows isn't an option, even if they weren't painted shut from the outside. My geriatric windows are the kind with the pulley structure inside the frame. The counterweights that are supposed to achieve the raising and lowering are AWOL somewhere in a channel below the windowsill. I take down the renovation list that's attached to the front of the fridge with the peach-shaped magnet and write "get new windows" on the bottom in red pen.

***

I'm going to Denver. Well, sort of Denver. Of course I don't get to go to real Denver. *Colorado Springs,* Robin said on my voicemail. *Not the easiest place to get to unless you drive, but I've found you a commuter flight out of Denver. There's only one flight there and back a day. Better not miss the flight or you'll be a tortilla!*

At least I'll get to see some of Colorado because I'll have to hang around Colorado Springs for a while since my flight back won't be leaving until late afternoon. Maybe I can find something to do there that will count as having been in Colorado so I can justify the fridge magnets I'm going to buy. Robin must have been reading a Fodor's guide to figure out how to get me there, because he also adds some fun facts about Colorado Springs. It's one of the most active lightning strike areas in the U.S. and that's why Nikola Tesla built and operated an experimental wireless power station there in 1899. It has the Peterson Air Force Base, the Schriever Air Force Base, the Cheyenne Mountain Air Force Station, and the Air Force Space Command. Evidently, these are responsible for intelligence gathering, space operations, and cyber missions. Somehow, I don't think these are places I'd be able to visit unless I flew in on an alien space craft.

I've made up the rules: anywhere I land is fair game for a magnet. Even if I've only ever been to the Seattle airport, that counts as Seattle, and I have the magnet to prove it. It's a stylized depiction of Seattle at night featuring the Space Needle. Apparently, it's a mini version of Toronto's CN

Tower (or maybe the CN Tower is a maxi version of the Space Needle) in downtown Seattle. I'll have to take the magnet's word for it.

There's also a message from the HVAC guys. *We've ordered the new AC unit, but they're back-ordered for the next two weeks. Have a nice day!* I guess that means I'll finally get air-conditioning when hell freezes over, at which point I won't need it.

When I get to Denver, I board a minivan from the main terminal (or DEN as non-amateur travellers call it) to the Rocky Mountain Metropolitan Airport, which is a corrugated-steel building about the size of a double garage. Inside, there's a small counter and six stackable plastic chairs that used to be white. A large, very flat, horizontal scale like the kind they have in a vet's office to weigh dogs (no way a cat could ever be weighed that way) stands to the left of the counter. I present my ID to a man wearing an RMMA uniform and tell him I'm on the flight to Colorado Springs. He nods and types into a desktop computer. A dot matrix printer dutifully spits out a piece of paper. He picks it up, folds it in half, scrawls something on the upper left corner, and points toward the scale.

I pick up my bag and prepare to weigh it. This is the first time I've ever had my carry-on weighed. "No," he says. "I need both you and the bag." This is also the first time anyone has cared about my body mass, which clocks in at just over 100 pounds on a good day. I don't think I'll be the person to tip any weight limit over the edge, but I follow the instructions and receive a notation on my boarding pass that I assume means I've cleared this gauntlet.

I guess I was early, because more passengers are now in the RMMA sanctum and I see I'm now back in the amateur ranks, because once they enter the garage, they immediately head to the scale, lug themselves and their stuff onto the weigh scale platform and yell out the total to the check-in guy. "220! 178! 192! 165!" They are all guys, of course. I wait and watch as I bide my time in the plastic chair before I begin what I hope will be an uneventful voyage.

They call the departure of the flight, and we file out the door behind the check-in desk to greet a Cessna twelve-seater. The guy that was behind the desk scrutinizes each boarding pass, then directs everyone to a seat. "You," he says to me. "In the middle. And put your laptop bag in your lap." This is different. Normally, the bag is supposed to go under the seat. But never mind. He directs the other passengers to strategically chosen seats and consults with the pilot, who sits in plain sight at the front of the plane. All seems in order, because we begin to taxi to the runway.

I can see the Rocky Mountains on our left as the tiny plane rises toward them. I don't know how it will possibly make it over the mountains, but that's not my problem. That's the pilot's problem. But we do rise and rise and rise and I get a great view of Denver as we motor south to Colorado Springs. Our flight time, according to the pilot, will be eighteen minutes. No need to get any work out. No time for anything other than admiring the view.

27

After the Colorado Springs interview, I catch a cab to the airport and work away at writing the case study while I wait for the flight back to Denver. It's the same drill as last time: everyone gets on the scale and the guy at the counter writes down the numbers. Not surprisingly, it's all the same people who were on the flight this morning. You'd think they could just use the weights from that trip, but maybe they want to allow for what we might have eaten for lunch, which in my case was a sad granola bar that got stuffed in my bag a few weeks ago for situations like this. I still weigh in at 102.

Instead of an electronic display showing arrival and departure times, there's a blackboard beside the check-in desk, which has clearly had a substantial number of erasures. There is only one departing flight — ours — and the current chalk announcement says it will leave at 18:05, which means two more hours in this plastic chair. I continue consulting my notes and tapping away on my laptop. I'll have this sucker written up in no time.

I'm still immersed in my perfect prose when I hear some grumbling from the guy sitting next to me. I look up and see that the counter agent is at the blackboard, writing something new. It's like watching *Wheel of Fortune* as we wait to see what will appear. Are we going to win or lose? Not a hard question to answer in the context of airports and airplanes. I'm guessing lose.

The departure time of 18:05 has been replaced with TBA. The counter agent surveys his handiwork for a few moments, then picks up his mic. "Folks, we have some weather. We're watching the radar and just as soon as we get a window of opportunity, we'll leave. Please stay in the lounge because when we go, we'll have to go quickly," he says. That won't be hard because there isn't anywhere else to be except in the lounge.

There's a lineup at the two payphones on the wall, but I don't need to be anywhere or call anyone, since the cat is highly unlikely to pick up the phone. Three passengers are consulting with the desk agent, who's shrugging his shoulders. They huddle, then pick up their stuff and leave the terminal. I hope they don't know something I don't. Maybe they just decided to drive back to Denver. It only takes an hour.

There's nothing else to do but go back to my Word document to review what I've written and start on the spreadsheet. A little while later there's an announcement. "We are boarding right now! Select any seat you want," the agent says as he shoos us out the door that leads to the tarmac. I take a seat over the wing and, because nobody tells me not to, stow my laptop bag under the seat in front of me. I'm barely buckled in as the plane starts down the runway. We take off at a very acute angle, directly toward the mountains.

The plane skims over the peaks with what looks to be about one foot of clearance, like a limbo dancer clearing a pole with no margin for error. The pilot makes no announcements. I guess he's too busy at the moment, because now we're winding our way through a field of thunderheads, threading the needle between angry grey cotton batting. I cinch my seat belt even tighter and close my eyes. Best not to look. This should all be over in eighteen minutes. The sound of the Cessna's engine is actually kind of soothing, like white noise. Or at least that's what I convince myself.

My stomach registers it before the rest of me. A sudden drop that feels like several hundred feet. Everything that's loose flies up to the roof of the cabin and then succumbs to gravity. The briefcase belonging to the guy across the aisle comes crashing down on his head.

Still nothing from the pilot. I can see him fiddling with dials as we continue to bump along. Finally, the pilot speaks. "Sorry about that, folks," he says, "that should be the worst of it. I'm already in contact with the Denver tower and we're cleared to land in five minutes." The supposed five minutes feel like two hours to me, but we are eventually on the DEN tarmac.

When we reach the gate, instead of the typical leaping to their feet and rushing to the door, everyone stays in their seat for a long time. Thankfully, my laptop and the draft of my case study are intact. I'm not sure if I would be more pissed off to be dead or if I had lost several hours of work. The guy across the aisle's computer didn't fare as well and neither did his forehead. He's dabbing at a trickle of blood, shaking his head, and muttering something about driving next time.

While I wait for my flight home from Denver, I compose an email to Simon to tell him about Homestore.com, the company I interviewed, yet another virtual venture. I see a theme emerging here. Seems like the online companies want as little physical presence as possible and to own as little infrastructure as possible. That way, when they go belly up, they can disappear in a puff of smoke and there's nothing to sue. But I don't mention this theory to Simon. Instead, I say I think we're safe because Homestore.com makes their money from advertising and subscriptions and seems to run a lean ship. The IT guy I met with was very proud of their postage stamp–sized office space. "Everyone still expects an address," he said. "This was the smallest we could find." I also don't mention the flight from Colorado Springs to Denver. He'd assume I'd driven.

28

I'm on the phone with Robin, amazingly in real time, arranging a set of flights for next week. "How did you make out with Rocky Mountain Air?" he says. "I hear it can get pretty rough."

No point in showing weakness. "It was fine. Very efficient," I say.

"I don't think Simon will be happy with the cost, though," he continues. "He's been hammering me to keep the travel expenses down. With five or six people on the road every week, it's starting to add up."

Sure enough, an electronic missive from Simon shows up the next day. *Everyone: As of next week, for any trip that is three hours or less by car from an airport, Robin will book you a vehicle via Budget. If you are not already a member, make sure you enroll in Fastbreak before then. Thanks for your cooperation in keeping costs down and profits up.*

I weigh my options. I'm okay for next week because I'm going to Cincinnati. I could quit the project, but that would mean leaving a bundle of case studies on the table. I could come clean with Simon and tell him about the driving thing, but maybe he'd fire me, leaving a bundle of case studies on the table. Doesn't seem to be a way to win this.

***

AAA-OK driving school (at the top of the driving school listings in the *Yellow Pages*) says they can help nervous drivers. I hope their definition of "nervous driver" includes people that are paralyzed with fear when they get behind the wheel.

My driving instructor's name is Mario. He looks like he's about eighty years old, and his plaid shirt and baggy beige pants look about that old too. He tells me he's a retired taxi driver. I'm not sure if that's good or bad. The car that's going to coax me into driving competence is a four-door Toyota Camry with the requisite driving school vehicle warning sign in fluorescent orange.

Mario gets out of the car and says we'll start with the exterior portion of the first lesson. We circle the Toyota while he explains the mirrors, the windshield wipers, the door handles, and the trunk. He opens the trunk and shows me the spare tire and jack. "Do you know how to change a tire?" he asks. "I wouldn't let my daughters get their licences until they knew how to change a tire." Perhaps I should walk before I run, Mario. Let's start with me successfully piloting the car on the road.

Once we're done admiring the capabilities of the outside of the car, Mario gets in the passenger seat while I get behind the wheel. The passenger seat isn't really just a passenger seat though, because Mario has a full set of controls on his side. We sit in the driveway as he leads me through adjusting the seat, the rear-view mirror, and the side mirrors. Then he explains the controls on the dashboard and how the automatic gear shift works. Finally, he points out the accelerator and brake pedals. Most of this stuff I remember.

After our interior orientation, Mario looks at his watch. "That's all the time we have for today. Tomorrow we'll drive." If he thought I would complain about having a driving lesson where I didn't actually drive, he's mistaken. I get another day's reprieve before I'm forced to face my nemesis.

The next day we start slowly by driving through some quiet residential streets with lots of stop signs. This gets me used to moving my foot between the accelerator and brake. So far, so good, Mario. Then we move to streets that are a little wider, with turn lanes. It's like riding a bicycle after years of not riding a bicycle. My driving reflexes are coming back. This is a piece of cake. I don't know why I was worried about driving. Then I feel the brake kick in. Only my foot isn't on the brake.

"Didn't you see the school zone sign?" Mario yells. "You were going sixty in a twenty zone." Okay, maybe I am a little rusty. Mario calls it a day. "Tomorrow we're going to do some highway," he says.

Mario selects a highway that's only barely a highway: Lakeshore Boulevard, a four-lane road with a fifty-kilometer-an-hour limit that runs between the big concrete pillars that hold up an expressway overhead. I discover that although I seem to be okay on streets with one lane going in each direction, having a car beside me freaks me out. Or even one behind me that's on my bumper because I'm daring to keep to the speed limit. Reflexively, I hug the side of the roadway. On go the brakes again.

"You were about to crash into that pillar!" yells Mario. "And you're going so slow the guy behind you almost rear-ended you!" Uh, Mario. You're the one who slammed on the brakes. "Okay, we're done. I can't afford to smash up this car," he says. "I'll refund your remaining lessons. I've never seen anybody so bad! No sane instructor would teach you!"

I'm tempted to point out that the reason I'm a bad driver is because I need lessons and if I'm not getting any better, perhaps he's not a very good teacher. But I need a lift home, so I keep my thoughts to myself.

29

The U.S. customs hall is surprisingly empty for a Tuesday morning, Tuesday being vastly preferred to Monday if you can help it, so those in the know try to arrange not to fly out on the first day of the week. As a self-defeating consequence, Tuesday can be pretty busy as well.

An agent who looks kind of familiar waves me over to his post. I plop my documents on the counter and assume a blank expression. He picks up my passport, opens it to the front and spends what seems like five minutes comparing my face to the photo. Then he reads each page excruciatingly slowly, scrutinizing each stamp and making notations in an official-looking black book with a U.S. coat of arms on the cover. I guess that's what happens when it's a slow border-crossing day. Luckily, I have lots of time to make my flight.

He finally finishes examining my credentials but does not give them back. Then he types something on a keyboard. I can't see his screen, though, because it's hidden from me by a black plastic shield that's attached to the side of the monitor. He types some more. I catch myself biting the nail on my index finger and hastily take it out of my mouth. I will my hands to behave, but then my right foot starts tapping. The border agent looks up from his keyboard.

"Looks like you travel to the U.S. very regularly. Way too regularly because we have no record of issuing you a B-2 visa. Can you please explain?"

I rack my brain for what I'm supposed to say. The letter Simon gave me is somewhere in a pile of paper on top of my desk at home. I haven't brought it with me since the first two or three flights because I haven't needed it. I guess that's the rule. The time when you don't bring the thing you always bring but never seem to use is the time you'll really need it. Maybe I've taken travelling light a little too far. How much room does a piece of paper take up? I ask myself a few more rhetorical questions, which do nothing to help the situation, while the border agent stares me down.

"I'm Canadian," I say, which is already made abundantly clear by the cover of my passport but allows me a moment to stall while I compose a more sensible sentence. "I am doing some research in the U.S. that will be compiled and sold to Canadians." Not quite true, but how is he going to know who's going to buy the report? "I'm paid by my client in Canada." In U.S. dollars, but why does he need to know the particulars? "I have a letter from the company I represent that explains this." Somewhere in my house.

The agent retains his iron grip on my travel documents with one hand, while the other hand one-finger pecks at his keyboard. Unlike me, I guess he didn't think Grade 9 typing was more important than Latin. Or do they even teach Latin in U.S. high schools? Latin sounds very unlikely. French, too. Maybe they don't teach typing, either. I promise myself not to ask him any of this.

A second agent arrives at the desk, and I suspect I'm about to discover the true curse of a slow day at the immigration hall. The first guy hands him my passport and boarding pass and tells me to follow him to secondary inspection. So much for ample time to make my flight. We walk along a narrow corridor lined with posters warning of dire consequences if you transgress the rules and regulations of entry to U.S. soil. One shows a man being led off in handcuffs while a woman holding a baby looks on in despair. *Twenty years to life if you forge travel documents!* Another shows a photo of an open suitcase stuffed with sausages and cured meat. *Fine of up to $10,000 for importing products not approved by the USDA!* Yet another has a picture of the Statue of Liberty and says, *We protect our citizens from threats by foreign powers!*

I take stock of my situation. My travel documents are bona fide, as far as I'm aware. I have no meat in my briefcase, as far as I'm aware. And, I am hardly a dangerous foreign power, as far as I'm aware. The agent ushers me into a small conference room with a frosted window. I'm relieved it doesn't also have bars and that the table and chairs aren't bolted to the floor.

"I'm told you've been going across the border very frequently," the second agent says. "Can you please tell me why?" I repeat my previous explanation, as verbatim as possible in case they had recorded my interaction with the first agent and were trying to trip me up. The second agent peruses my passport carefully, making notations in his own copy of the official booklet, then picks up my boarding pass. "You are coming back today?"

"Yes," I say. "I'm on a tight deadline to get this research project done. I make my trips as short as possible. I do the interviews and fly right back home."

"Why can't you just do them over the phone," he says. Why indeed? I don't bother explaining Simon's edict. Instead, I tell him the interviews get very technical and the company often has to show me things to explain about their operations so it's impossible to do them on the phone. I hope I didn't make that sound like I'm a spy. Looks like I'm okay because he moves on to his next question. "Do they ever give you samples you bring back across the border? Like intellectual property that could be duplicated?" Oops. Maybe he does think I'm a spy.

"No," I say. "I wouldn't be able to bring it into Canada anyway. If I haven't been out of the country for more than twenty-four hours, I can't bring anything back." I think that's sort of the rule. Shouldn't he know the rule?

"Really?" he says. "That's pretty backward. U.S. citizens can bring up to a thousand dollars worth of goods any time."

"Yes, we really are strict," I say. "Maybe that's why we don't have all the innovation you have in the U.S." Did I go too far with that?

Apparently not. "You're allowed in today," he says, "but be prepared to produce your permission letter next time. I've made a note on your file." Great. I now have a "file." He hands back my documents. I walk briskly toward the immigration hall exit and start to sprint once I clear the glass doors leading to the gates.

30

The sign as we're leaving the airport says, "Welcome to Kentucky." This is a bit disconcerting since I'm supposed to be in Cincinnati, which I'm pretty sure is in Ohio. I mention this to the cab driver.

"Ha!" he says. "A lot of people get confused. I think they put that sign up for a joke. Cincinnati's right across the Ohio River from Kentucky. You'll see when we get downtown. The airport's on the Kentucky side." Good to know. I hope they have Kentucky fridge magnets at the airport. I can add another state without having to really go there. Still the story of my trips so far. Kind of going places, but not really. "If you go the other direction, you'll be in Indiana," he says. Maybe they'll have Indiana magnets too! A trifecta of states in one fell swoop.

We cross a bridge over a span of water that looks like it's less than a mile wide and arrive at *The Cincinnati Enquirer* building, which is right downtown and directly across from the river. There are riverboats, the kind with the wheel at the back, tied up on both shores. The cab driver tells me there have been steamboats on the Ohio since 1811, travelling from Cincinnati down to St. Louis, and New Orleans on the Mississippi. He points out the art deco high-rises that face the water. "Just as fancy as Chicago," he says. I'll have to take his word for it. Chicago will probably not be on my itinerary because it's a place people actually want to go to.

The antique office building that's my destination has a lobby with more gilt embellishments than Buckingham Palace. The marble floors act like mirrors and the real mirrors on the oak-panelled walls are as big as billboards. The elevator door has silver-coloured panels etched with peacocks. Or maybe it's actually silver. I press the button for the seventh floor.

The elevator opens directly into a busy open newsroom full of desks populated with people on the phone, or stabbing at keyboards, or scribbling in notebooks. About half of them are smoking. I look around to see if there's a receptionist or some other way to announce my arrival. I wave to try to get the attention of one of the reporters, to no avail. Everyone is studiously ignoring me. I check the time on the large clock on the wall and see I'm exactly on time. I figure if I stand here long enough, someone will become aware there's a strange red-haired girl in their midst.

Then I notice a shelf near the door and a sign that says, "Oink for service." Next to the sign, there's one of those horns like you see on a clown car, the kind where you squeeze a rubber ball and a noise comes out of a thing that looks like a funnel. I scan the room again to see if anybody's in eyeball range. Nope. I guess I'll have to do the squeeze thing. "Oink oink oink" is the noise it makes. Thankfully, this gets some results. One of the reporters puts down his cigarette and gets up from his desk. "I'm here to see Jeff," I say. "And nice oinker!"

He laughs and tells me Cincinnati's nickname is Porkopolis. "We're the pork capital of the Midwest." Bingo. There's my Cincinnati falcon. He walks me to an interior conference room and tells me he'll go and get Jeff. A few minutes later, a man who must be Jeff enters the room. He's wearing a short-sleeved dress shirt with a pocket protector that holds three pens. He puts a sheaf of computer paper on the table, swivels a chair around and sits on it backward.

"Our paper was founded in 1841," Jeff says. So far, I'm gathering that the past is very important in Cincinnati. Maybe it's an inferiority complex. When you're even smaller than Cleveland, that's got to cause some city-esteem issues. I settle in to hear the details of the *Cincinnati Enquirer*'s ASP project.

Jeff tells me he's the webmaster for *Cincinnati.com*, the online version of the *Enquirer*, which was launched in 1996 and originally called *Enquirer.com*. "We were early to the game," he says. "We had no idea what we were doing, but we knew we needed to do it before someone else snapped up our URL name." He recounts the growing pains of going online. "We have electronic archives going back to the paper's inception and hundreds of thousands of web pages. The problem is nobody could access them effectively." I can certainly see how that would be a problem.

Then they got a new search engine, hosted by an ASP, and now life is good. I walk him through the costs and benefits. When they initially set up the website, they included a comment function that would send an email to Jeff. "Every single one of those emails said, 'your website sucks'," he says. I'm tempted to summarize the main benefit as "having a website that doesn't suck," but I don't think that's going to fly. I make a note in my notebook anyhow. Maybe when all this is over, I'll compile a list of ASP interview greatest hits, just for fun. My notebook is full of stuff like this. You couldn't make it up if you tried. Especially the oinker.

31

I arrive back in Kentucky and make my way through the airport to the shopping concourse near the gates. It's actually a pretty nice example of an aeronautical terminal, and by now I have a pretty robust basis for comparison. There are tall, arched windows that let in lots of natural light and a lounging area populated with white rocking chairs that have wide, flat arms and fan-shaped backs. That's definitely something unique.

I locate the Hudson News store and poke about the fridge magnet display. Alas, there's nothing related to Kentucky nor Indiana, so I'm stuck with Ohio in general or Cincinnati in particular. Should I choose one that shows a riverboat? One that shows an art deco office building? One that features the cast of *WKRP in Cincinnati*? Then I see it. A metal silhouette of a pink pig. It says *Cincinnati*, not *Porkopolis*, sadly, but it will do.

I go back to the concourse lounge area and manage to snag one of the rocking chairs. I had to get up really early to make my flight and then I had to face the border guard interrogation and stress out about whether or not I'd actually make it to Cincinnati. I'm exhausted. The rocking chair moves gently and rhythmically, in contrast to the bustle of people rushing to gates or walking purposefully toward the baggage claim area. I have about an hour to kill, so I take my notebook out of my bag to review what I captured in the *Cincinnati.com* interview.

I wake up with a start. "Flight 564 to Toronto. Final boarding call," the loudspeaker says. I grab my laptop bag and start what's becoming a familiar sprint in what I hope is the direction of the gate. I arrive drenched in sweat just as the second-last person to board the plane clears the glass doors. I find my seat, plop down, shove my stuff under the seat in front of me, and fasten my seat belt. Ever since the Colorado Springs incident, I tighten the belt aggressively and never ever take it off during the flight. Better to be uncomfortable than sorry.

Once we're at cruising altitude, I fish my bag out from under the seat and reach inside for my notebook. It doesn't seem to be in the main pocket, nor behind my laptop. I lift the flap that seals the outside pocket and check that. Nothing there except granola bar crumbs and my passport. I rack my brain. Did I leave it in the conference room? In the taxi? At security? Then I remember. I had it when I was at the rocking chairs. And I don't have it now. I must have dropped it when I stood up to run to the gate. Not only do I not have my Cincinnati notes, I've lost all the notes I've taken so far.

I sigh so loudly that I startle my seatmate. "Long story," I say. I lean back into the headrest and close my eyes to preclude any conversation. I have no words, anyhow. Literally. My notebook had the words. All of the interview content, for sure, but also my side notations and falcon ideas and doodles that may or may not have been brilliant case-writing prompts. If this was the movie of my life, it would be a major crisis point. The music would be melancholy. Instead, I ask myself what Gloria Gaynor would do. I hum "I Will Survive" as I recap in my head the important parts of the Cincinnati interview, get out my laptop, and start typing.

***

I can hear the phone ringing as I unlock my door. I almost trip over the cat as I dash to the kitchen. His priority is dinner. Mine is intercepting the phone call. I lose. I let the machine answer while I dish out tuna cat food that smells disgusting. When the cat is satisfied with my service, I press play. I'm not surprised when it's Simon's voice.

We just had a status meeting on the ASP project. Two things. We need to pick up the pace to make sure this thing is done and dusted by the end of September before our year-end. Also, we need to keep tight control on expenses. I get paid on profit, you know. Anyhow, Robin's going to run all travel costs by me for pre-approval. Let me know if you've got questions.

As far as I'm concerned, my pace has been pretty good. Until now. I didn't get *Cincinnati.com* done on the plane and I'm going to have to listen to the full recording several times to recreate my notes. That's going to take a few days at least. Plus, I'll need to burn a couple of hours going downtown to my favourite stationery store to get a new notebook, because not just any notebook will do. I need the kind with tabs so I can separate my interviews, and it has to be smallish so I can stow it in the front pocket of my laptop bag. And it has to be red or pink. My mojo insists.

But it's the travel thing that's most worrying. Simon will notice if I don't book a rental car when I'm supposed to need one. I contemplate this as I drain the water from a can of tuna on top of the food in the cat's dish and make myself a tuna sandwich. Hopefully I'll still be eating real tuna instead of cat food in the near future.

I retrieve the *Yellow Pages* from under the phone and open it to driving schools, once again. This time, I navigate to the end of the alphabet, in case the schools that start with an "A" all know each other. I write down the number for Zebra Driving School. I'll call later, I promise myself. I have more important things to do right now, like clean the cat litter and defrost the freezer and organize the basement.

32

Fred, my new driving instructor, doesn't seem as scared of me as Mario was. Maybe that's because his car is a Lada that couldn't get more beat up if it tried. In the manner of people looking like their dogs, Fred seems to have taken on the visage of his Lada. Or maybe it's vice versa and he went looking for a car that was pretty much his twin. He has about three days of beard growth, and a Band-Aid that was fresh about a week ago graces the bridge of his nose. I notice the fingers of his right hand are bound together with a bandage at the knuckles. His hair is collar length, and I would bet this is more because he never bothers to get it cut than any sort of fashion statement. His clothes are my first clue: grey t-shirt with grease stains and khaki cargo shorts that hit just below the knee.

When he picks me up in his sad Soviet conveyance, he tells me we're going to go up to the big IBM parking lot at Don Mills and Eglinton. "We'll take some turns around the lot and I'll see where we're starting from," he says. I already like his approach much better than Mario's. I won't need to actually drive on any roads during my driving lesson.

When we reach the parking lot, Fred stops the car in a far corner and tells me to take the wheel. We each walk around the car to change spots. "Just do a tour of the lot," he says. I put on my seat belt and hit the gas pedal. "Whoa, stop!" he says, as we lurch forward. "Aren't you forgetting something?"

I don't think there's a speed limit in parking lots, but when was I last driving in a parking lot? I rack my brain. I do have my seat belt on. I have demonstrated that I know where the gas pedal is. What else could it be? I deflect by trotting out that old joke. "Hey Fred, why do we drive on a parkway and park in a driveway?"

"Not funny. First thing when you get in any car that's not your car, or even a car that is your car, check that the seat is positioned so you can reach the pedals. Check that you can see out of the rear-view mirror. Check that you can see out of the side mirrors. Check that you know how to use the windshield wipers. Check the gas gauge. Check, check, check, check, check! It's the only way to avert disaster, especially with rental cars. Are you expecting to drive rental cars?" So many things to know. So little I wish to know. So little time to learn the things I have zero interest in knowing.

I tell Fred the kind of true reason for needing lessons. Keeping my gig and all that. Except I explain my nervousness by saying I'm worried about driving in the U.S. Do they drive the same as in Canada? "Pretty much," says Fred. "Except they honk more and give you the finger more and take up more space. You're going to need to sharpen your elbows."

He tells me to drive back to the entrance of the parking lot and pull up to the curb so we can switch spots. I aim the car more or less parallel with the concrete lip and am delighted when I stop with barely a whisper between the passenger door and the ledge. "Good try," says Fred, "but I do need to be able to open the door. Back it up and give it another go."

I congratulate myself on getting the car into reverse without looking too long at the letters on the gear shift, back up a few yards, and add a wider berth as I approach the curb. This time there's ample room to open the door. Maybe even room for two doors. I look over at Fred for the approval I deserve. "That's okay, I can walk to the curb from here," he says.

***

As usual, I can hear the phone ringing when I open the door after Fred drops me off. As usual, I'm too late to intercept the call.

Hi! It's Holly! You're going to Shreveport. It's in Louisiana. It's probably no Las Vegas, but it's supposed to have a casino. Robin says it's kind of hard to get to and based on my experience lining up the appointment, the guy you're going to see sounds a little weird, but I'm sure it'll be okay once you get there. We're picking up the pace. Your bum will be on a plane twice a week, minimum.

Beep.

Robin here. Shreveport. It's in Louisiana. I think they have a casino or something. Holly says the guy you're going to see sounds a little weird. It's a little hard to get there. I can send you through Dallas or route you through Chicago and Houston. You know the new policy. Gotta go the cheapest way. My bonus is on the line here.

Am I the only one with no bonus on the line? Oh, wait. Forget about a measly bonus. My entire fiscal future is on the line. *And I'll book you a rental car to get to your appointment,* he continues. *Shreveport doesn't seem to have a taxi stand at the airport. It must be pretty small.*

33

For our next lesson, Fred says we're going to Rosedale. He has the same outfit on as last time and I'm pretty sure it hasn't been washed. Or possibly he swaps out one equally squalid set of clothes for each day of the week. I can't decide which option I'd prefer. Better to let my imagination rest. Rosedale's just a quick hop to the west, over the bridge that spans the Don Valley Parkway. It's a four-lane thoroughfare that people treat like a raceway, so thankfully Fred takes the wheel until we get to the residential neighbourhood. As I suspected, my elbows are still too round.

We quickly reach a quiet, leafy enclave with large stone mansions set well back from the road. There are no sidewalks on the winding streets and no evidence of human inhabitants. Just black squirrels frolicking on manicured lawns and hopping across wrought iron fences to feast on artisanal walnuts from massive trees. Life here is lived at twenty-five kilometres per hour.

I cruise as sedately as the ambience encourages, stopping at stop signs, signalling my turns, and checking my mirrors like a pro. I could drive all day if all driving was like this. I settle into a groove, my inside voice congratulating me on my emerging expertise. Why did I avoid driving for so long?

"Whoa," says Fred. "Were you not paying attention? You just blew through that stop sign. You must observe your surroundings at all times. Good thing there's never any cops around here. They're too busy policing the speeders on the Viaduct. Enough of this walk in the park. Next time we're going to drive in some real traffic. Take it up a notch. Your elbows will thank you."

I'm spending more time with Fred than anyone else these days. Except for Holly and Robin, who I don't really spend time with as much as trade frantic voicemails with; however, I admit the frantic bit is always mine. I'm grateful that Fred is always gentle with his feedback, but, in line with his perpetually bruised knuckles, he doesn't pull punches when I ask a direct question about my driving capabilities. I tell him I'm going to have to drive in suburban Shreveport. "Not on an actual highway, I don't think," I say. "Am I ready to do that? Where would you put me on a scale of one to ten for my driving excellence?" I am well aware of my tragic flaw. Be the best at whatever I do. I spent many hours I'll never get back striving to be a professional figure skater, an award-winning actress, a prima ballerina. None of these endeavours ended well. And neither did my feet. But that's not Fred's concern.

He ponders my question for a minute and says, "About five-point-five out of ten. We're going to have to spend a bunch of time on left-hand turns. And merging. Merging will be key. When are you leaving?"

"Tomorrow?" I say, with hideously apprehensive upspeak. We haven't done any of those things yet.

"Okay," he says. "I guess a verbal tutorial will have to do. Get out that notebook that seems to be attached to your hip. Start writing."

***

I'm trying something new with my travel packing. It's even more minimalist than the male road warriors. If I'm just going overnight, I stuff a pair of underwear in my laptop bag and just wear everything else on repeat the next day. I'm pretty sure this will be revolutionary. Maybe I'll end up in the travel wardrobe hall of fame.

My route to Shreveport is as circuitous as promised. I have to change planes in Dallas, which gives me time to stop at Hudson News and pick up a fridge magnet. I plunk a miniature blue cowboy boot with a spur on the heel that says "Texas" on the counter and zip open my bag to rummage for my wallet. The clerk does not disguise her annoyance as I dump the contents onto the counter. Notebook, tape recorder, pens, black bikini underpants, wallet.

I look over my shoulder and see a line-up forming for the cash. The guy behind me is reading the back cover of *Who Moved My Cheese?* and the guy behind him seems to be deciding between a container of cashews and a bag of black licorice. Nobody noticed my unmentionables. I sweep everything except the wallet back into my bag, pay for my magnet, and scuttle out of the store.

I'm consulting the departures sign for the location of my Shreveport gate. "Excuse me, miss," someone behind me says. "Is this yours?" It's the guy who bought *Who Moved My Cheese?*, waving a Canadian passport. I unshoulder my laptop bag and open the flap. No passport.

"Yes," I say. "Probably. Thanks. Must have dropped it." I snatch the passport from his grip as politely as possible. At least he wasn't holding my underwear.

When I get to the gate, I board a smallish plane that's thankfully larger than the one that almost took me to Augusta and way bigger than the one that narrowly managed not to kill me in Colorado. I notice the cabin is mostly empty, which is probably a clue to the popularity of Shreveport as a destination. There's no entertainment system, but there is an in-flight magazine in the seat pocket that's probably meaty enough to amuse me for the hour it's going to take to get there from Dallas. I flip through the magazine, which is mostly ads for restaurants and attractions in the destinations served by this regional airline, but it also has a feature on Shreveport. My lucky day.

The magazine tells me Shreveport is the third largest city in Louisiana, after New Orleans and Baton Rouge. I have, of course, heard of New Orleans, but it seems like pretty slim pickings after that as far as Louisiana metropolitan areas go. Apparently, Shreveport used to have a thriving oil and gas industry that somehow went bust and has since turned to gambling as its economic engine. The article quotes the mayor as saying "our city continues in its efforts to revitalize its infrastructure, revive the economy through diversification, and lower crime. We've been doing real good chasing them gangs out of town. This last year our crime rate was only sixty percent higher than the rest of Louisiana." I'm pretty sure this remark reveals everything I need to know about Mr. Mayor and his town.

As we start our descent, the flight attendant makes an announcement. "Welcome to the tristate area, where Arkansas, Louisiana, and Texas meet. And good luck in Shreveport!" I hope she means good luck at the casinos as opposed to something else. And is everywhere in the U.S. in a tristate area? Probably not. Just the scintillating places I get to go. I remind myself of the fat invoice I'll get to send after this trip and leave the plane to see what Shreveport has in store.

The terminal is a small rectangular building with vinyl siding that looks like it started out black a long time ago but is now several shades of grey. There are two gates next to each other, neither of which has the technology that attaches a gangway to a plane. Instead, they roll up a staircase. I retrieve my bag from under my seat and head out, excited to experience the wonders of Louisiana's third-place metropolis.

34

I shouldn't have been worried about how to find the rental car desk. It's right there, next to the café that has a display of wieners rolling under a heat-lamp behind glass and is beside a bank of slot machines. I approach the counter, rummage through my bag to find the reservation confirmation Robin emailed me, and retrieve a crumpled piece of paper. I slide it along with my driver's licence across to the guy manning the desk. I hope he can't tell by looking at it that all it's done for most of its life is sit in the junk drawer in my kitchen.

"This looks like you," he says when he picks up the licence, "but where in the heck is Ontario?" I point to the small type in the upper right corner of the card that says Canada. "Canada! My goodness. That's a long way from here. Didn't know you even had many roads in Canada. You sure you really know how to drive?"

I don't answer that question because I don't know how else to get around Shreveport and I can't afford to miss my appointment. I just stand there with a neutral expression. Maybe he doesn't think I speak English either. As if to confirm my supposition, when he hands me back my licence and the rental documents, he tells me to wait a minute.

He walks over to the café and grabs a napkin, brings it back to his counter and gets a pen out of his shirt pocket. He draws me a map while explaining very slowly, with no big words, how to find my car. When I exit through the front door of the terminal, I'm not surprised to see that no explanation was required. The row of rentals is lined up on the left and couldn't possibly be closer to the entrance of the building. They are all pickup trucks.

My particular pickup truck is mostly red except for the rust around the wheel wells. It has some kind of rack on the back of the cab and, as any guy I know would be able to tell, it looks like the business end could hold many sheets of drywall. I unlock the driver's door and haul myself up behind the wheel. I unzip my bag, slide out the piece of paper with my MapQuest map and directions, and contemplate the task at hand.

First, I review the advice Fred gave me at the end of my lesson. "Get yourself an SUV or a minivan whenever you book a rental car," he said. "You sit up higher in those so you can see everything that's going on. Plus, you'll be bigger than regular cars and they'll stay out of your way. Hopefully." Well, I guess a pickup truck counts in this instance. Anyhow, the Lada drove like a tank (not that I had any basis for comparison to driving an actual tank). How different could a pickup truck be? Fred also told me to always back up very slowly and stick strictly to the speed limit. "In town, you can even go a little under what's on the sign, if that's what makes you comfortable. Don't try it on the highway, though. You'll get creamed!"

I review the route that will take me to Kendrick Tax and Accounting. Looks straightforward enough. A right turn out of the airport, then a right on Hawthorne Drive, then another right at the lights onto Hush Puppy Grove, then a final right to get me to 21 High Roller Avenue. If that's not a lucky address, I don't know what is. It doesn't immediately sink in that all these driver-friendly right turns will reverse themselves into nerve-shredding left-hand ones when I return to the airport.

I insert the key into the ignition and reverse slowly out of the parking slot onto the road that will get me out of the airport. Thankfully, the late-morning traffic is light. Hawthorne is a residential street that looks like the best a real estate agent would be able to say about it is that it has "excellent proximity to the airport." There's a row of tiny bungalows with barely the thickness of a newspaper between them. Each front yard has a discarded appliance or piece of furniture. A wringer washer, an upholstered rocking chair, a box spring with sprung coils.

As I continue toward Hush Puppy Grove, I notice something else: groups of men sitting on stoops idly watching the traffic or sitting on upholstered rocking chairs on the lawn or using appliances as bar tables. Maybe not discarded after all, just outdoor furniture. As I pull up to a stop sign and wait for other cars to do their thing, one of the bystanders yells "Nice gun rack, Red!" I'm not sure if he's referring to the colour of my hair or my truck. At least I now know what the thing on the back of the truck is for. In the rear-view mirror, I can see eyes following me as I accelerate through the intersection. I'm tempted to floor it, but instead I follow Fred's speed limit advice. If jail is bad in general, I'm sure a Shreveport jail is a whole different situation.

The address on High Roller is a two-storey building with a sign in front listing the offices inside. Kendrick Accounting is in suite 103 on the first floor. I park the truck, walk up three steps, and enter through a glass door. Suite 103 is to the left and I can see a woman with a beehive hairdo and cat eye glasses working at a desk behind another glass door etched with the name of the company. I push on the handle and nothing happens. I switch to pulling, in case that was the problem, and it still doesn't budge.

At the sound of my door wrangling, the woman looks up. She holds up her index finger and then presses a button on the side of her desk. The door buzzes and I can hear it unlatching, so I push the door and enter the office. Once she determines I'm completely inside, the woman presses the button again and the door locks behind me. "Can't be too careful around these parts," she says. "Some people think accountants look after money. Well, I guess we do look after money, just not actual money. Once they break in, they figure that out, but not before they mess up the office."

The office is crammed tightly with two wooden desks, several swivel chairs also made of wood, a tower of bankers boxes, and five grey metal filing cabinets. A desktop computer and a small laser printer are balanced on a workstation table at the back of the room. "My husband just ducked out to get a haircut. He should be back in five minutes." Maybe he wanted to look extra sharp for our interview. Or maybe time is a fluid concept in Louisiana. "I can show you around the office in the meantime." There doesn't seem to be much to reveal other than what I can already see, but I nod my assent to the fifty-cent tour.

Mrs. Kendrick points out the obvious things. But this is a chance to do something productive with my wait. I ask her to explain the computer set-up. "Well, if you think it's crowded in here now, you should have seen it when we had the IBM AS/400 and that big honking printer in here. I don't know what Bill was thinking with that one." I don't know what Bill was thinking, either. A server room in a third-rate office building in a dicey area of Shreveport? But maybe every area of Shreveport is dicey. I need to make sure to get the full IBM story when Bill finally shows up.

There's a rap on the glass door. Mrs. Kendrick bustles back to her desk and presses the magic button. Looks like even Bill doesn't have the power to open the door from the outside. I wonder how they get into the office when they get here in the morning?

Bill's about sixty and is dressed exactly how a Shreveport accountant should dress. I can see red suspenders peeking out from the jacket of his blue and white seersucker suit. He takes off his straw fedora and places it on the top of a coat rack near the door. His recent haircut is as short as a new marine recruit's. "Hi, I'm Bill Kendrick," he says.

35

I didn't have high hopes for the Kendrick Accounting case study. How exciting can accounting be? But it turns out Bill managed to manufacture plenty of excitement for his sole proprietor business. And contrary to another accountant stereotype, Bill could spin a fine yarn.

Back in 1983, he had a client in the software business who had developed an accounting package for oil jobbers. The jobbers, he told me, buy gas in bulk then resell it. Anyhow, Bill struck a deal with his client: modify your software so I can use it to automate my business and in exchange I'll keep your IBM computer in my office.

It seemed like a good idea at the time, but like the sorcerer's apprentice and his enchanted broom that wreaked havoc, it did not achieve the desired results. Before long, Bill had an entire computer room and two line printers. "Line printers are those big things that crank out the stripped computer paper," he said. I don't tell Bill I have a PhD in line printers, having worked in the industry that eventually spawned ASPs, because I don't want to get him off on more of a tangent than he's already on.

"Do you know how much of a racket those things make? I was a full-time accountant and a full-time computer operator." In comes the ASP, the magic spell that's proliferating the computers is broken, and Bill lives happily ever after. And there it is. The falcon.

I was going to talk about Shreveport and gambling and try to connect it to accounting, but this is miles better. The Goethe poem that Disney's *Fantasia* based its sorcerer's apprentice story on ends by saying something like "only a master should invoke powerful spirits." I think I'm going to win falcon of the year with that one. Computers as powerful spirits. ASPs as masters, doing things clients shouldn't attempt themselves. The triumph of twenty-first century technology. Poetry in motion.

I unlock the truck and get ready to make my way back to the airport. I review the route again. A left, a left, another left, and another left. I hear Fred's voice in my head: "When you wanna turn left, turn your signal on as soon as you can. You gotta check all directions and all your blind spots." If only I could remember where the blind spots are.

I manage to get out of the Kendrick's parking lot without incident. I congratulate myself for my skill, ignoring the fact that there are no other cars on the road so skill has nothing to do with it. The left onto Hush Puppy is a four-way stop sign deal. When I pull up, another car has just arrived on the other side of the intersection. We do our polite do-si-dos and another successful left turn is in the bag. Fred would be proud.

The intersection of Hush Puppy and Hawthorne is two lanes each way with a traffic light. As soon as I can see the lights in the distance, I put on my left-turn signal. Just like Fred told me to. There are many more cars here, probably also going to the airport, but I've got that lucky truck advantage. I can see.

The car behind me honks his horn. My big rear end is probably blocking his view of the traffic signal. Too bad for him. He should get a minivan. We pass a few more side streets and the idiot behind me keeps honking. I finally get to the light and wait for it to turn green. Wonder of wonders, it has an advanced left-turn arrow. I sail on through and continue on to the airport. The guy that was honking turns as well, then guns it over to the right-hand lane and gives me the finger as he passes me on the inside. Asshole.

I leave the truck where I found it just outside the airport, pat it on the hood, and head for the check-in gate. Strangely, there are very few other people in the terminal and no line-up. I plonk my driver's licence on the counter with new pride. Now it's not just for ID! I tell the clerk I'm on the two thirty flight to Toronto via Dallas. "Oh. We cancelled that flight," she says. "Didn't have enough passengers. Next one is at eleven tonight. If we get enough passengers."

What? I'm stuck in Shreveport for nine more hours? says my inside voice. My outside voice thanks her profusely, in case there's a politeness lottery to get a seat on the red-eye.

I haul my stuff over to the bank of payphones near the café, which probably still has the same wieners basking in orange light. Maybe they're permanently the same wieners, since someone would only buy one if they were desperate. I dial Robin's eight-hundred number. It rings and rings and then goes to voicemail. I leave a useless message.

Robin, you have to get me out of Shreveport! They cancelled the plane. I'm at the airport. Next flight's practically tomorrow.

I sit down on the floor beneath the payphones and rest my back against the wall. I decide I'll try him every fifteen minutes. An hour later, I've left four more messages. I notice a few more people have come into the terminal. Hopefully, that means there's a flight to somewhere sometime soon. I go back to the counter and wait in line. When I get to the front, I ask the clerk what the next flight is. "Houston," she says, pointing to the one departing flight on the board. At least Houston isn't Shreveport. I compose my face into my best pathetic-businesswoman-trying-desperately-to-get-home-to-my-nonexistent-kids smile (the looking pathetic part not being much of a reach). I ask her nicely to move me from the Dallas flight to the Houston one.

The Hudson News has the usual array of self-help books. *The Power of Now. Don't Sweat the Small Stuff. Who Moved My Cheese?* I notice the latter title has a new location on the top-ten shelf. I hope it likes it there. The magnet selection is meagre, but I do score a clip that has a magnet on the back half, and on the front, sealed clear plastic, containing glitter and a loose pair of tiny dice, against a background that says, "Welcome to Fabulous Shreveport." It will indeed hold my grocery list fabulously.

I eat a hot dog as I sit in the departure area. Who knows when food will next make an appearance? And who knows what I'll have to sort out once I get to Houston. If I get to Houston.

36

I arrive back in Toronto from Shreveport via Houston and Chicago at three in the morning. The airport is not a happy place at three in the morning, mostly because of all the unhappy people like me, running on empty, which my stomach is actively reminding me is actually better than succumbing to another dubious hot dog. Despite the rain, my cabbie makes quick work of the deserted highway and dark streets because he's going about twice the speed limit. Fred's taught me to pay attention to these things. "Whatcha doin' coming home so late? You don't even have a fancy dress on," says the driver. He's no Harry Chapin, that's for sure. And he will not get to keep much of the change.

When I finally get home, the cat's snoozing on the porch furniture and ignores me as I try several times to select the right key in the dark. Before I head upstairs, I rummage through my laptop bag, retrieve my magnets, and position them on the fridge. Aside from my Shreveport souvenir, I also have one from Chicago that's supposed to evoke the wind, and one from Houston that depicts oil wells. I haven't yet decided how I'm going to end up organizing them. By location? By colour? By shape? It didn't occur to me when I started the magnet thing that my fridge will forever remind me of this project. I'm not sure yet whether or not this will be a good thing.

Quelle surprise, the light's flashing on the answering machine. I bundle up a stinky dish of rejected cat food and listen to the first message.

Hi! It's Holly! You're booked for South Dakota the day after tomorrow. The company sounds kind of weird. I hope Robin's on the case. He isn't returning my emails or calls. When's the day after tomorrow? Is today tomorrow or is tomorrow tomorrow? How do you even get to South Dakota? Am I going to have to get myself to South Dakota? Isn't Mount Rushmore in South Dakota? I stop asking myself questions and start writing down the rest of Holly's message. I'm going to some kind of bank in a place called Brookings. Details to follow. I'll let her sort it out.

Beep.

Robin here. Got your messages. I was out with stomach flu. Norovirus. Nasty. You do not want it. Did you get back from Shreveport okay? I should leave Robin a voicemail right now and say I'm in Houston racking up hotel costs because I can't get home. Or better still, tell him I'm in the casino in Shreveport and taking another flight back because I'm on a roll. Then again, I want to keep on Robin's good side. He's helping me rack up the Marriott points. And I need him to figure out how to get to Brookings, South Dakota, which I'm guessing he'll say is hard to do.

I haul myself up the stairs and flop down on the bed. I still need to crunch the numbers for Kendrick before I can send it off, but most of it is done. I never thought I'd be so thankful for airport downtime. Time well wasted, indeed.

"Brookings is not the easiest place to get to," says Robin when he calls me mid-afternoon. What else is new? I'm sure the other people on this project take non-stop flights to places they've actually heard of. "You're going to have to stay two nights. I think first prize would be one night in Brookings.

Ha! I'll route you through Minneapolis to Sioux Falls, then you'll drive to Brookings. The good news is it's not winter." He goes on to tell me there is no Marriott in Brookings.

"The best I can do is the Econo Lodge. It gets two stars, probably because it has an indoor pool. Those people in South Dakota must love being able to swim in the winter. Come to think of it, they probably can't swim in the summer either, unless it's not snowing that day." He snorts at his joke then tells me he'll email my itinerary. After I hang up, I realize I forgot to ask him if today is tomorrow or tomorrow's tomorrow. I need my tomorrow. I need Fred.

***

When he picks me up, Fred's in fine fighting form. "Challenge day," he says. "Gotta knock more chunks off those elbows."

"Um Fred," I say. "I'm going to South Dakota in a day or two. I'm pretty sure I'll have to drive on a highway. Am I ready to do that? On a scale of one to ten, what's my new level of driving excellence?"

Fred ignores me, gets out of the car, and opens the passenger door. "You're driving," he says. "We're going to go across the Viaduct and down Parliament, turn left on Lakeshore and take the ramp to the Gardiner Expressway. Then we're going to go east to the Don Valley Parkway and north to the Bloor Street exit. No skill rating until we've done that. And I'm not going to say a single thing until you're right back here in front of your house."

37

The Sioux Falls airport, I notice, has wieners luxuriating under a sunlamp, exactly like the ones in Shreveport. But they can't fool me. Much like my previous middle-of-nowhere experience, the rental car desk isn't hard to locate. Right there beside the hateful hot dogs.

I confidently march up to the counter and present my credentials. "Canada, eh?" the guy says. I smile. No banjos here. Just a mutual respect for the dangers of snow machines and blackflies. "Okay. We got you a regular four-door compact. Automatic transmission and everything. Since yer Canadian and ya know 'bout this stuff, that's all's we got 'til huntin' season, when we got a few pickup trucks. Ya don't need a pickup truck, do ya?" I tell him I'm happy with whatever they have. I don't tell him that having no pickup trucks is actually a bonus. Especially if they come complete with gun racks.

He hands me a set of car keys and points me to the rental parking lot. "Any of 'em will work with these keys. But wait a minute — gotta give you the safety briefing. Okay. The car has the normal block heater, plug it in when you get where you're going so the battery'll start in the morning. Oh. That's just the winter instructions. Never mind. I'm supposed to tell you all this stuff anyhow. The snow brush is in the back seat. The emergency foil blanket is in the glovebox. We don't supply emergency chocolate bars anymore. People just kept eating 'em." Isn't that the point with chocolate bars? I don't say that out loud, though.

"It's the Datsun," he says, and points me toward a row of five identical brown, boxy four-doors at the side of the terminal building. They look like they rolled off the assembly line in the 1970s. The kindest thing I can say is they look almost serviceable if you squint. In addition to both starting with an "S," Sioux Falls and Shreveport have even more in common than I thought. Airport rental cars are not their strong suit.

I check the MapQuest route I printed out to give me driving directions from Sioux Falls to Brookings. The map shows a line that goes due north 57.2 miles up the I-29. I think that's about a hundred kilometres. Not a single turn, left or otherwise. I head in the direction of the highway, and as MapQuest pretty much promised, the road sign says Brookings is sixty miles away. But I don't understand why my printout says it will take me about forty-five minutes to get there. For sixty kilometres, maybe, but surely not miles. I guess I'll find out.

I pull onto the interstate with a few other cars that immediately leave me in their dust. Then I see the speed limit sign. Seventy miles per hour. Last I heard you could only drive fifty-five in the U.S. Maybe South Dakota is a renegade state or maybe I'm way behind the times. Regardless, there's no possible way I can manage seventy. That's way too fast. But I hear Fred's voice caution me. "Never go below the speed limit. You could cause an accident because everyone's expecting you to be doing at least the speed limit. Usually ten percent more, if you wanna know the truth."

The Datsun shakes as I timidly press down on the accelerator. The speedometer needle inches up from fifty-five to sixty. My hands grip the steering wheel like I'm holding on to the edge of a cliff to avoid certain death. Cars continue to whiz past me in the left lane. For some reason, they're all Datsuns. At least I sort of blend in. Maybe they think I'm having car trouble. That gives me an idea. I turn on the hazard lights. Thank goodness Fred told me what hazard lights are.

I continue turtling toward Brookings, getting waves and what I hope are friendly honks.

South Dakota is so flat they can probably see next month's weather coming. I've looked on the map and the state is as square as a piece of Shreddies, with a grid road pattern subdividing sections that are as precisely laid out as the pieces of a prairie quilt.

An hour after I leave Sioux Falls, I arrive at the intersection of Highways 29 and 19 where the Econo Lodge is located. The confluence of the highways creates four impeccable right-angle triangles that look like they were crafted by a geometry set. In fact, everything I've seen of South Dakota so far is a drafting student's dream. As flat and even as a piece of Bristol board.

The Econo Lodge parking lot is full of Datsuns. I make a careful note of where I park. If the same key works for all of them, I might accidently drive off with the wrong one. On second thought, that's not the worst thing that could happen. Someone could drive off with mine. Just in case, I take all my worldly goods out of the car.

I obtain my room key from the front desk and head down a dim hallway shod in faded red swirly patterned carpeting. I've learned from all my forays so far that hotels favour swirly patterns. This one has vastly surpassed its quota of sins to hide. The décor of my room continues with the red swirly theme. I pick up a brochure from the top of the dresser and peruse the hotel's vast amenities. The pool, of course. And there's a restaurant. And at one point there must have been a casino, but now there's a big black "X" through the description.

The Econo Lodge's restaurant is called the 1429 Roadhouse, which is baffling because it certainly was not established in 1429. And it's located at 2515 6th Street, so I don't know exactly what they were going for with that name. However, it appears to be my only dining option. It has the obligatory wagon-wheel light fixtures hanging from an acoustic tile ceiling that's decorated with water stains and remnants of tobacco smoke. I take a seat at a wooden stool on one side of a U-shaped bar. The bartender looks my way and waves a menu. I nod and scan the room. A few old guys are playing shuffleboard and a family is finishing a basket of chicken fingers. Then I see something in the corner that looks like a stash of NTN Playmakers. It's Tuesday. This may redeem boring Brookings.

"Do you guys have NTN?" The bartender tells me they do and hands me a Playmaker along with my Caesar salad with chicken and a glass of water with lemon, no ice. I raise the device's short rubber antenna, press the on button, and log in. Before the game starts, the TV screen shows only the list of players in the bar. For now, Elvis is alone. If it stays this way, I'll be in a good position to win the bar. And get a free glass of water with lemon.

38

I spoke too soon. A group of about ten guys just walked in and commandeered a table with a good sightline to one of the TVs. They're laughing and ribbing each other. Maybe they've just come from playing ball. There are certainly enough major league jerseys in evidence. I just hope they won't be too noisy. I'll need to concentrate on my game if I want to end up on the North American rankings, so my team back in Toronto will see me on the board. Elvis is in the room.

But then the bartender grabs the rest of the Playmakers and brings them over. Uh-oh. Maybe trouble is afoot. He comes back to the bar and begins filling draft glasses and mixing rum and Cokes. There's no question these guys are regulars. He puts the drinks on a tray and ferries them over. I can hear the conversation they're having with him loud and clear.

"Where's the other Playmaker, Jim? We're missing one," one guy says.

The bartender points in my direction and shrugs. "Not my problem, Pete. She was here first."

Ten heads turn to look over at the bar. "Ah, it's just a little red-headed girl. And she's by herself. Probably never played before and doesn't even know how it works. Nothing to worry about. Two of us can double up. Let's get on the board. The game's starting soon."

"Who are you, Pete? Charlie Brown?" one of the bros chimes in. Much laughter ensues. I'm glad they're having fun at my expense. Women in a restaurant alone are fair game, I'm learning. That's why I always sit at the bar. So the bartender can be my bouncer.

The bartender returns to his post and begins drying glassware. "Jim," I say (because now I know his name), "what's with those guys?"

"You are in the presence of greatness. That's The Borg. You know, after that hive mind thing from Star Trek. They're all big Trekkies. Played here for going on five years. Ranked in the top ten for North America ever since. They sure weren't happy you snagged a Playmaker. But hey, ten against one. And just a girl at that. No contest."

The Borg! Wait 'til I tell the guys I've met The Borg in beautiful Brookings, South Dakota. At least I get to leave. They're stuck here working at whatever drudgery they work at. That thought buoys my spirits. Why not give them a run for their beer?

The NTN warning clock is ticking down rapidly. The warm-up round is about to begin. It's usually pretty easy, but just ten seconds to answer each of ten questions, so speed counts. I position my fingers on the numbers one through five on the top row of the keyboard. We learned typing by touch on manual typewriters that had no letters or numbers on the keys. Our only aid was the poster that rolled down in front of the blackboard that showed an intact alphanumeric layout whenever the teacher decided to throw us a bone — which was almost never. My finger reflexes are well honed. My gauntlet is down.

I breeze through the warm-up, but it's only worth five hundred points. I also see The Borg has captured the full bounty. Pocket change. The Countdown round gives a bit more breathing room, at fifteen seconds to answer, but the longer you take, the fewer points are up for grabs. Starting with this round, there's a list of five possible answers on the screen. The wrong ones disappear gradually until just before the fifteen seconds expire, then only the correct one is left. Theoretically, it's possible to swoop in and change your choice. but it'll only snag you a few measly points. Speed continues to be of the essence. I'm confident my secret powers will prevail.

The first Countdown question comes up on the screen.

Who won Superbowl XXXV?

Not only does this have to do with sports, my second worst subject, it also involves math, my worst subject. Math with Roman numerals, no less. The list of options shows five cities: New York, Pittsburgh, Dallas, Baltimore, and Miami. At my opponents' table, I hear someone shout out, "Team has it. The Ravens." This is of no help to me. Then I hear another guy say, "Really? It was Baltimore? I thought the Giants pulled it out at the last minute. But maybe I'd had too many brewskis by then."

I press my finger on the number four, while they continue to discuss. As the answer choices diminish, I see I've chosen correctly. For full marks. The table full of self-professed geniuses argued until the last minute, then rang in at five points. They look up at the leader board, then over at me. "Guys," one of them says, "you can't be shouting out the answer. There's an enemy in our midst."

"But that's how we do it! So everybody gets the right answer quickly!" another guy says. "It's our Borg advantage!" Not anymore, suckers.

But now it's the Category Quiz. There are two category options to choose from, but you have to vote and the majority wins. Today's categories are sports and television shows. I select television shows, knowing it's probably a spoiled ballot against a table full of guys who are honour bound to choose sports. Not that I'm great at television shows, but at least I've seen a few of them. Sporting events, not so much. I watch the screen to see which category is about to disappear. I can't believe it when television is victorious. This does not bode well. It must mean they have some TV show experts on the team. And now it dawns on me that I've successfully stopped them from revealing the answers.

I do miserably on most of the questions, which all involve shows I've never heard of. *Blossom*? Is that about a flower shop? *Wasteland*? Was that set in Brookings? *Robin's Hoods*? Are you kidding me! *Beastmaster*? I can't begin to figure what that one was supposed to be about.

I'm relieved when we reach the final question in the round. I don't need more humiliation.

> "Believe it or Not" was the theme song for this television show.

Ha! I know this one, but only because of another television show. George riffs on it for his answering machine message in a *Seinfeld* episode: "Believe it or not, George isn't at home." I select *Greatest American Hero* and manage to pull fifteen hundred points out of my butt.

I limp through the Lightning round, where speed is of the essence (my fingers are accurate, my answers not so much) and the Pyramid round, which relies on getting all five questions right to acquire twelve thousand points. It's the cash cow of the whole tournament. And for some reason, all the questions are about animals. I'm doing pretty well so far, but no better than the guys. The fifth and final question arrives.

> Horsetail is a _____ that is considered a living fossil.

The bartender has stopped wiping the counter and is eyeing the game. "No doubt they'll get this one," he says. "They've got a botanist on their team." I look at the list of options. *Cloud. Insect. Grass. Mold. Lizard.* Only one could be in the realm of botany. Apparently, there's more than one source for an answer reveal. I earn the full twelve thousand points, along with many withering looks from my fellow competitors.

The Final Strategy round is just one question and you get to wager your entire bounty, but only before they reveal the question. What the heck. I go all in. And wait for the reckoning.

The banana belongs to this family.

The options on the screen are: *Maundiceae, Malivaceae, Musaceae, Mcarthuriaceae,* and *Mazaceae*. I suppress a guffaw as I select *Musaceae*. The guys are arguing loudly about this one.

"I know it starts with an M and ends in 'eae'," say the Pete guy.

"No shit, Sherlock," says one of his peeps. The bickering is heated and snarky.

There are many things I could say to gloat, like *resistance is futile* or *I am the beginning, the end, the one who is many* (or at least able to defeat the many). But I don't. Then I feel something hit my head and land in my lap. A spitball. Followed by several more that pelt my chair and the surface of the bar. The bartender tells them to settle down. The grumbling persists, but thankfully the spitballs do not. Jim gives me a voucher for a future free meal for winning the bar. "Can't comp you on the water," he says with a laugh.

39

MapQuest says the company I've come to visit in Brookings is less than a mile away from here, just over the highway bridge and a few blocks south. It doesn't say how feasible walking is, but I'd rather get some fresh prairie air than drive. I'll let my car hang with his homies.

I walk through the Datsun-filled hotel parking lot and set out on the road toward the highway overpass. There's a narrow sidewalk on the bridge that's maybe more of a wide curb than a place people are expected to walk. I remember my Elmer the Safety Elephant rule, *where there are no sidewalks, walk facing traffic*, so I keep to the left-hand side. The drivers of the endless stream of Datsuns driving west look at me quizzically as they make their way to work, but they're driving pretty sedately, probably because their geriatric cars are exhausted from trying to make it to seventy miles per hour on the interstate. But after successfully piloting my bicycle through the treachery of downtown Toronto for decades, this is as benign as vanilla ice cream without the vanilla.

After the bridge, I take a left to leave the main drag and walk down 22nd Avenue South to my destination, a squat office building that holds the headquarter of Sunshine Savings and Loan. Not surprisingly, their parking lot is full of Datsuns too. Folks around these parts evidently don't need to spend much time deciding what car to buy. Nor pick the colour. This must be what parking lots look like in Russia. If they have parking lots. Fred's Lada would be like the fabled ugly duckling here. Striving to obey to conformity but sticking out like a shiny object in a sea of mud.

At the lobby desk, I ask for Peter Nordstrom. The receptionist stops chewing gum long enough to take my name and hand me a parking pass. "Hang this on the rear-view mirror of your Datsun," she says. I slide the pass back across the desk and tell her I walked because it's so close to the hotel. "You walked?" she says. "Geez. You're brave. I'll buzz Pete."

A few minutes later Peter's assistant shows up to escort me to his office. South Dakota summer female fashion seems to involve polyester pantsuits in pastels and hair secured by scrunchies even though the apex of their popularity was in the last century. I probably look far too urban in my black suit and red ballet flats. But I'm not here for a sartorial showdown. I'm here to pocket twenty-five hundred dollars U.S.

The assistant ushers me into a big office that's aggressively undecorated with anything that looks fancy. Metal filing cabinets. Fake wood desk. Vinyl office chair mended with duct tape. One of those gooseneck desk lamps that I often see at the curb on garbage day, wishing for a forever home to save it from the landfill. A green blotter that holds a mug that says *I'd rather be golfing*, stuffed with a bunch of pens.

There's a separate computer workstation in the corner. The CPU sits under the desk and there's a bulbous monitor on top. The floor is clad in carpet tiles, the kind where individual squares can be swapped out if needed, without having to replace the entire carpet. The whole place smells vaguely of takeout pizza and stale donuts.

"He's just wrapping up the mid-week sales meeting," the assistant says. "Can I get you a coffee?" I tell her I don't drink coffee and I'm fine. I can imagine the lunchtime gossip among the scrunchie crowd. She walked here? She has no Datsun? She doesn't drink coffee? I take out my brand-new notebook and arrange my tape recorder on the edge of the desk.

I take a stroll around the room to peruse the decorations on the walls. They certainly don't not fall into the category of art. Maybe it's meant to be tongue-in-cheek. Or perhaps it was selected with great care to fit right in with the sofa that's upholstered in an orange and brown plaid made from some substance not found in nature. Behind the desk there's a print of dogs playing poker. There are certificates and awards from the Association of State Savings and Loans. And there's a photo of a bunch of guys wearing identical ball caps that appears to have been taken at the nineteenth hole of some golf club. I take a closer look at the logo on the hats, in case it's something I can use as an icebreaker. It says "NTN." I quickly resume my seat and assume a neutral expression. Surely, this must be a coincidence.

A few minutes later, Peter Lundstrom enters the room, apologizing for his delay. "Mid-week numbers are important," he says. "Sets the stage for Friday. And end of day Friday sets the stage for open of business on Monday. A lot of stuff has to happen on the weekend to make Monday morning dawn with sunshine. Oh. Hi. I'm Pete." At which point he looks at me more closely.

"I know you! You're that chick that was at trivia last night! Where the heck did you come from?"

"Canada," I say, and smile and say nothing more. I have nothing to explain. If there's anything I've learned on this journey, it's to shut up and let them talk. As predicted, Pete eventually can't stand my silence.

"Okay. This ASP thing. We're going to be a case study, right? Published and everything?" I nod. Holding fast to my silent coercion. "Okay. I have the interview guide they sent me. Let's do this thing. I have to say, you were pretty good last night. Not all the guys think the same way I do, but beating someone fair is okay. Didn't think they had NTN up in Canada. But I guess you guys don't have too much else to do. Especially in the winter." I don't bother to point out that Brookings is pretty much at the same latitude as Toronto.

"Let's get started," I say.

40

Sunshine Savings and Loan's mission appears to be to find money where the sun don't shine. Pete tells me their ASP software has revolutionized their business model. "To be honest, payday loans and short-term financing are our bread and butter. With our new system, we can now charge interest by the minute. You can imagine how that might add up!" He says this with unbridled glee. "So, on Wednesdays, we have a crystal-clear view of who might be going to default by Friday, and we can go ahead and slap on a lien or foreclose or whatever before midnight, collect the assets on the weekend and start liquidating on Monday!"

In my head, I'm already starting to figure out how to spin this so I can minimize the slime I'll need to wash off my body and maximize the chances that Pete will be happy to approve the case study. I'm going to go with the accounting angle. Just the numbers. No need to mention the good citizens of greater metropolitan Brookings and its environs whose finances get led to the slaughter every minute of every hour of every day.

I sit back and let Pete expound on his delight with his ASP until I'm sure I've gotten what I need. I'm finding it takes me less and less time to do the interviews. I can zoom in on the important things, pluck the nuggets (and the falcons) and get it done in under two hours. On the downside, on average it takes me two days' worth of travelling to get wherever I'm going and back.

When I finish collecting the requisite information and bundle up my stuff, Pete even seems to have warmed to me. Making people think you are paying attention to them and listening works every time. "Didn't see your Datsun in the lot," says Pete. I tell him I left it at the hotel because it wasn't far and I wanted to stretch my legs.

I hesitate to ask my burning question but decide to go for it. "What's with all the Datsuns?"

Pete laughs. "Nobody really knows the true story, but rumour has it that when Datsun phased out their brand in 1986, there was a huge surplus. Our governor found out about it and arranged to buy a bunch for cheap. I think that was kind of during oil crisis years and South Dakota being so spread out, lots of driving happens. They were good on gas. So, everybody who wanted one got a good deal. Now most of them are on their last legs." Tell me about it, Pete. "Anyhow, it's kind of a point of pride. We're all going to drive them into the ground. We should have the Datsun on the South Dakota flag."

This story kind of sounds a little fantastic, but maybe it's true. When I lived on the Prairies in the 1980s, they imported a bunch of Dodge K-cars that were ordered by Saudi Arabia and never shipped. They were exceedingly homely beige vehicles with no chrome on the outside (maybe because of the heat?) and bench seats both front and back. Turns out they performed brilliantly in the winter.

"Let me drive you back to the hotel," Pete says. "Not safe to walk. Hey, it's sports trivia tonight. All of The Borg will be there. You could sit in with us. Maybe be our lucky charm." Indeed, Pete. Luck be a lady tonight. Not this lady.

I politely decline. "Gotta start work on the case study," I say. "I'll get you something to review within a couple of weeks. See you on the NTN rankings."

Back at the hotel, I make a stop at the bar to order a free sandwich to go. I don't want to be anywhere near NTN games today. Back at my room, I unwrap my dinner, turn on the TV for background noise, and settle in to start writing. The news recounts the usual drivel that has nothing to do with anything or anywhere outside of the continental U.S.: Miss South Dakota visits a kindergarten! The president goes golfing! A dog falls down a well!

41

"What do you think about the marijuana thing?" says Fred. We're doing highway driving today, up the Don Valley Parkway to the 401, the major east–west artery. I'm pretty good on the DVP because it's always so backed up it goes about as fast as liver and onions at a greasy spoon diner. I'm not sure what'll happen when we merge onto the big highway, but there are lots of exits. Many opportunities to get off if I need to. At least that's what Fred told me when I reluctantly booked the lesson.

"You gotta do it sooner or later," he said. "You've been lucky so far, but I doubt that luck's gonna last. They've got them some big-ass highways down there."

"What marijuana thing?" I reply. I'm getting much better at talking and driving at the same time. Maybe soon I'll be able to listen to the radio, but not until I can pry one hand off the wheel while the car's in motion.

"It's all over the news. How can you not know? They've legalized it."

"Seriously? I'm pretty sure the U.S. news would broadcast that. They'd be afraid of stoned Canadians storming the border. Or Canadian pot cartels threatening life, liberty, and the pursuit of happiness."

"Well, not exactly legalized-legalized. Just for medical purposes. But still. I think I'll start developing back pain. Reefers must help with that and there's nothing they can do to prove you don't have back pain. Hey! Pay attention! Get over to the right! We're almost at the on-ramp." Well, almost good at talking and driving. Perhaps more practice required.

The 401's travelling at warp speed compared to the DVP. I hug the right-hand sound barrier and steel myself to venture into the frantic traffic that sounds like a freight train bearing down on a damsel tied to the tracks.

"Press the gas! Press the gas! Press the gas!" Fred says. "Don't go slower than the lane you're merging into. I've told you that a bazillion times." I manage to insert the car into the lane, but only because a pickup truck slows to let me in. Still, I think I've merged extremely elegantly, considering I haven't done this in a very long time.

"Good thing we've got the driving school sign on this thing," says Fred. Oh. I forgot about that. "Confidence, confidence, confidence. The three most important rules of driving."

"It's a little hard to be confident when it's possible, or in my case probably likely, that I'll kill myself or somebody else. You, maybe."

"Look, who's in charge here?" says Fred. I have no answer to this. Isn't he in charge? Who else could be in charge?

"You're in charge," he finally says. "If you're not in charge of the car, then nobody is."

Thanks for pointing that out, Fred. That means nobody is.

He allows me to get off the highway at the next exit but tells me we're going to keep doing it until I'm a 401 pro. I'm pretty sure that'll take the rest of my driving lifetime, at which point I'll have spent enough to pay for his kids' orthodontia, hockey gear, post-secondary education, and destination weddings.

When I get home, the red light is flashing, more than delighted to tell me I've received new phone messages. The play button produces Robin's disembodied voice.

Robin here. I've got you on an early flight to Evansville, Indiana. Direct via Air Canada. I thought it would be hard to get to. You'd better buy yourself a lottery ticket based on that one! I'd never heard of Evansville, Indiana, but never mind, now I have, whatever good that'll do me in the future. Just don't get stuck there. There's probably only one plane a week. Anyhow, then you'll drive to Henderson from there. Indiana? I thought I was going to Kentucky.

I climb the stairs up to my office, practically the most exercise I've managed lately, and tell my dormant technology to contact my friend MapQuest. Up he pops, happy to be of service. He practically gushes as he tells me I'm about to enter another tristate area! Henderson, Kentucky, is actually south of Evansville, Indiana. I'm not quite sure how that works, but I guess geography is immutable. It appears I'll be driving a rental car across the state line. Is that even allowed? Near as I recall from the TV shows I've seen in my U.S. travels, state lines seem to be like those invisible fences for dogs: the force field will bounce you right back where you came from if you contravene the rules of passage. I pick up the phone.

After the beep, I say "Sorry to call you after hours, Fred, but this is important. Am I allowed to drive a rental car across a state line? Please call me back. I'm flying out tomorrow. Early. I might be in trouble."

42

I'm completely confused. This morning, I flew into Indiana to go to a place that's in Kentucky. Fortunately, Fred left me a message late last night after I'd gone to bed.

Well, I looked it up and technically you're right about the state line thing, at least for Kentucky. It has something to do with hillbillies and shotguns and bootleg moonshine and fourteen-year-old brides. Near as I can tell, you aren't fourteen, don't have a shotgun, and probably aren't transporting moonshine. Just smile nicely when you pick up your rental car keys. And wear a suit. Definitely wear a suit. And some of them fancy girlie shoes with the pointy toes. Pointy toes'll distract the guy at the counter. No guy can resist pointy toes. Fred is clearly not allowing for female desk staff. And I'm pretty sure he doesn't speak for all men.

It would indeed be very inconvenient if I was thrown into a Kentucky jail. Or an Indiana jail. Or an Illinois jail. Despite Fred's advice, I didn't do the pointy shoes. Both because I am veteran of countless airport concourses and the fact that I don't own any pointy shoes.

I briefly wondered how they decide where to incarcerate you when you're caught doing something felonious in a tristate area, which gives me something to distract my anxiety with as I pick up my Indiana rental car. I present my best corporate self to the Budget desk and am given the keys without incident. No underage hillbillies to see here.

The road to Henderson is thankfully lightly travelled, so my knuckles retain a blush of colour. It follows the south bank of the Ohio River that looks to be less than a hundred feet wide as it meanders its way to join the Mississippi. It's a stretch to refer to the oozy, mousey, sludge as water. On the other side of the highway, there are rows and rows and rows of tobacco plants that appear to be at least ten feet tall with leaves like brownish-green elephant ears. They're interspersed with fields covered in delicate yellow flowers that resemble roses.

The town itself looks half-abandoned. There's a bunch of boarded up warehouses by the river and a structure that probably started out life as a mill. My MapQuest instructions say to turn right toward another group of ancient industrial buildings, clad in sooty red bricks, with nine-paned windows held together precariously with black iron. Fat chance they'd be able to let in any light, what with the coating of grime that's probably as old as the building. This is the world headquarters of Sights Denim.

When I open the door, I'm surprised to see the inside of the warehouse is actually kind of funky, kitted out like an artsy gentleman's club with curvy hunter-green leather couches, coffee tables made from steamer trunks, Navajo rugs, and boxes of Cuban cigars displayed on an immense bar cart. I look around to see if there's a reception desk, but all I see is a mahogany cabriole-legged table that holds a delicate silver bell beside a tent card that says "Ring, please." Much classier than an oinker, I'll give it that. I do as requested.

A youngish guy dressed in jeans (of course) and a black t-shirt appears from a doorway across the cavernous room. "I'm John, the IT guy," he says. "You must be from BDE." I nod my assent. He goes on to tell me he'll give me a tour of the operation first, then we'll stop in to talk to Bart, the owner of the company, and over lunch I can ask him any questions I still have. "We'll wrap up in time for you to catch the three o'clock flight."

He ushers me through an immense door that looks like it escaped from a barn. It opens on a room filled with industrial washing machines. "What we do here at Sights is after-market denim processing. Right here is where we do the sand-washing and stonewashing. You know about that stuff, right? Remember the eighties? It's all coming back. Not many people know we really do use sand for the sand-washing, but for the stonewashing, we actually use randomly shaped chunks of resin instead of stones. We found that out the hard way. Real pebbles can kill a ten-thousand-dollar washing machine in a nanosecond."

We walk into the next room, which houses devices that would not be out of place in the Marquis de Sade's dungeon. Workers are surrounded by boxes of jeans with various famous logos: Levi's, 7 for All Mankind, Ralph Lauren. I see them plucking pairs from the boxes and referring to instruction cards that must spell out the particular torture to be administered to the pants. Some get shredded in a very precise way, others get frayed or knee-capped.

"This is where much of the artisanal things happen," Josh says. "It can increase the value of the product by hundreds of dollars. Simply by destroying it!"

I think back to the first pair of Calvin Kleins I bought in 1980 that cost me sixty bucks. A fortune. I certainly wouldn't have paid more for them if they'd come complete with rips. But then again, I guess I'm no longer in with the in-crowd.

The third room is chock full of workers bent over tables shaped like large ironing boards, attacking jeans with sandpaper. "That's just regular old sandpaper," Josh says. "If you take a look at these distressed jeans," he says as he points to a pile of Levi's, "you'll see none of this is random. Each pair has exactly the same wear pattern. Each brand uses their own pattern, of course. They have to differentiate." I guess so, but I'm at a loss to tell the Levi's from the Laurens, and I'd like to think I have more than a passing acquaintance with denim.

In my early days of high school, girls were only allowed to wear skirts or dresses. Even in winter. In contrast, those with XY chromosomes were allowed to show up in casual pants and shirts without collars, until Grade 10, when jeans joined the acceptable trouser list, while the XX crowd were still stuck with cold knees. We did what any outraged teen would do in the early 1970s: held a sit-in. In front of the principal's office. For three days. Spoiler alert: we won. As a result, I never wore anything other than jeans until I got my diploma. And also well after that, as I made the rounds of more universities than is generally advised. By then, we'd moved on to overalls, the antithesis of designer denim.

"You're really going to enjoy Bart," John says as we continue on to the CEO's office. "He lives and breathes denim."

43

Bart's office is in a mezzanine overlooking the torture chambers. We reach it via a spiral staircase that would be completely at home on the set of *The Phantom of the Opera*. As if to prove me right, there's even a massive chandelier suspended from the rafters. His enclave is encased in glass and has the same furniture as the entrance lounge, except his couches are clad in denim. I'm not surprised by this, nor that he's also wearing jeans and a black t-shirt. The corporate uniform, it appears.

John introduces us, and Bart tells me how happy he is to participate in the study. "Our business has been completely transformed," he says. "You know, I've always loved fabrics," he says. "My mom used to take me to Bernstein's Men's Wear shop here in Henderson on the first day of every school year. She'd buy me three pairs of rigid Levi's with reinforced knees and I'd watch with amazement as they got broken in and changed as I wore them. Literally becoming a walking history of my experience and expression." I doubt he made up this little speech just for me. By now I've been the recipient of enough CEO origin speeches to spot them at twenty paces, but I must admit I've never thought of jeans that way. Bart just handed me my falcon, fully roasted on a spit. "I'd like you to truly immerse yourself in the product," he says. "This is what those delicate yellow cotton flowers become. Like butterflies emerging to spread their wings at an all-night rave party."

I think that metaphor is not only mixed, but mixed up, but at least Bart has explained those fields of yellow flowers. He continues. "John'll escort you to the sample room. Take whatever you want. Give me some feedback. Thanks for coming."

"Wow. That's cool," says John as we make our way down the stairs. "Normally just staff gets free product." We pass through several dim corridors and eventually end up at a room that's at the back of the warehouse. It looks just like a denim store at the average mall, with piles of jeans in racks and on tables, plus change rooms at the back. And a sign that says, "Out of Sight." "Everybody can come here once a month to take whatever they want. All our employees are brand ambassadors," John says.

The company store also seems to have its own sales clerk. A woman looks up from a computer monitor as we approach her desk. "Hey Josh. Just running the sales figures for last month. I love our new software!" Josh tells me her name is Jen. "Size twenty-seven?" she says. I nod. "Okay. We've just got some hot new styles. Just go on in and I'll bring you a bunch."

I spend the next half-hour doing a fashion show in front of the fake-store mirror. I will be too cool for school when I get back home with my bleeding-edge designer jeans. At the end of my non-shopping frenzy, there's a stack of a dozen pairs that Jen has deemed essential. Then I remember I have to cross the border. After less than twenty-four hours. No jeans for me. I thank her and explain to Jen that, alas, I'm from another country.

"What? Jeans aren't allowed in Canada? I knew you guys were a little backward, but I didn't know you couldn't wear jeans. Wow." I spell out the customs thing as clearly as I can. Using short sentences.

"Well. Here's what you do then. Just smuggle them. What's the worst that could happen? They'll throw you in jail?" I don't tell her the worst that could happen is I'd never be able to cross the border again and not be able to finish my case studies and have to eat cat food. But designer jeans that retail at about two hundred bucks each? Maybe I can make an exception. Since Jen has volunteered to be my partner in crime, I rise to the occasion.

I figure I can manage two pairs. We decide to wrap the sand-washed Levi's around my laptop and, with only a few advanced Tetris moves, manage to cram the bundle back in the bag. It's definitely stuffed, but no bulkier than most guys' laptop bags that typically have so many electronic doodads hanging out of them, it looks like they're planning to start their own offshoot of RadioShack. Since it's so hot, Jen suggests I sequester the artfully distressed Ralph Laurens inside my suit jacket and carry it over my arm. Larceny in motion.

On the drive to the airport, I rehearse what I'm going to say when I go through security, since I'm going to have to extract my laptop from amidst the pants and put my suit jacket in the X-ray bin. Will they even care about free-range jeans? Is there such a thing as a jeans-bomber?

But I needn't have worried. All the security guy did was remark on how light I'm travelling. "You frequent flyers are getting smarter all the time. Just between you and me, I can't stand those amateur travellers with all their carry-ons," he said, as he handed me the bin containing my two pairs of contraband denim. Maybe I should call Simon and tell him I must no longer be an amateur. The security guy said so!

When the flight attendant distributes the customs form prior to landing, I only hesitate briefly when I put a check mark against "Nothing to declare." I'm a little disappointed when I don't have to explain myself to the customs agent. "Just travelling light, officer. On the road every week. Have you heard of the Travel Wardrobe Hall of Fame? I'm nominated this year!" But my carefully crafted speech isn't required. He barely glances at my form as I pass out of the baggage hall with my bulging laptop bag, suit jacket situated over my arm.

Ricky is characteristically cranky when I get home, asking me loudly why he's outside when the food's inside. I don't remind him that he was insistent on going out when I left this morning. And that there are perfectly good mice hanging around the garage. He dashes into the kitchen, complaining about the malnutrition clearly evidenced by his twelve-pound body. I appease him by opening a can of something suitably smelly before getting the machine to tell me who wants to talk to me.

Hi! It's Holly! Guess what? Got you booked for Thursday. You're going to Henderson. Another weirdo! I'll get Robin on the case.

Henderson? Doesn't she know I was just in Henderson? Maybe it's an old message that's somehow resurrected itself. And that reminds me. I haven't heard from Simon in a while. Could be a good thing or it could mean there's a shoe that hasn't yet dropped.

44

When I extract my freebie jeans from my laptop bag, I discover several fridge magnets that still haven't made it to the fridge. This includes a buffalo that says South Dakota and a mini version of Mount Rushmore. Some people might think that one is a bit of a cheat since I never got even close to Mount Rushmore, but in my opinion, it personifies South Dakota. Also, there were no Datsun magnets. I also have one from Indiana (a corn field) and Minnesota (the shape of the state, crowned with a moose), because passing through this many airports deserves a badge of honour. Or at least a magnet of honour. I situate them on the dwindling fridge real estate and stand back to admire the display.

It reminds me I've spent too much time sitting on planes and in cars. Surely, I'm allowed to go for a run even though it's the middle of the day. I pull on my Lululemon capris and a tank top, unearth my battered runners from the coat closet in the kitchen, and head out for a fast-paced tour of the neighbourhood. I'm not surprised when the flashing red light greets me when I get back and I'm not surprised when the message is from Simon. A shoe has indeed dropped but in a good way.

I'm sure you're on the road. We're getting close to wrapping up the data-gathering portion of this project and I have some very good news. There's an ASP conference the week after next. All of our sponsors will be there. Holly's going to line up a few interviews for you. Plus, you can meet with many of them to get final sign-off on a bunch of the case studies. It's a win-win-win! It's going to be key to meeting our deliverable milestones. Oh, and the best part is you get to go to Florida for three whole days! Orlando! The happiest place on earth! The clients are paying for your hotel and meals because you're a special guest at the conference. Maybe you can give them a bit of a status update too? Robin will be in touch re flight. They're comping that too! Safe travels!

This is the most enthusiastic Simon has sounded about a trip he's not going on. Shouldn't he be the one getting final sign-off and taking advantage of free room and board? Is this extra work even in my contract? Then I put ten and ten together. Orlando. July. A train wreck combination of family summer holidays and sauna-grade heat. On the plus side, I can knock off my final three or four case studies in one fell swoop. I'll reply to Simon after-hours and fill him in on my most recent triumphs.

But first I need to figure out what's up with Henderson. Of course, Holly isn't there when I call to ask for clarification. I'm sure her disembodied voice will eventually show up on my machine. In the meantime, Fred and I will attempt to conquer the 401 once more.

***

"Pity about that quintuplet," Fred says when I get into his Lada. I ponder this as I move the driver's seat forward and adjust the mirrors and secure my seat belt. What the heck is he talking about?

"You know, that bunch of girls that were born somewhere in Quebec in the nineteen thirties? One of them died the other day. I think a couple of them died before that. They were in a circus or something."

"No Fred, they were born in Corbeil. In Ontario. Kind of near North Bay. Kind of near where I grew up, sort of. And they were never in a circus. At least I don't think they were. Of course I didn't hear about it. I was in Kentucky and Indiana except I really only wanted to go to Kentucky."

I suddenly realize I'm saying all this as I back out of the driveway, cross the bridge and merge onto the DVP. I also finally clue into what Fred's up to.

45

My answering machine tells me Holly has indeed sorted out the Henderson thing.

Hi! It's Holly! You know how every state has a Springfield? Apparently, that's why the town in The Simpsons *is called Springfield. Could be anywhere. Seems like Henderson is also a Springfield. This time it's in North Carolina. Henderson, I mean, not Springfield. But it probably has a Springfield too. Robin's sorting it out. Who knows? Maybe your next trip is to one of the Springfields!*

And sure enough, Robin slides into my voicemail tape within the hour. *Robin here. You're going to fly to Raleigh. Henderson's a little hard to get to directly. I think it's north of there. Budget will have a map.*

I head up to my office to consult MapQuest. But Holly's made me curious. Before I dial up the driving directions, I ask the internet to tell me if there's a Springfield, North Carolina. Of course, there is. It's an unincorporated community in Gaston County, near the city of Gastonia. Good to know.

It appears that Henderson, North Carolina, is about sixty miles due north of Raleigh and it'll take about an hour and a half to get there on US 1, traffic permitting. This tells me the prescribed speed limit is somewhat more sedate than seventy miles per hour. Not that I'm complaining. I print the Henderson map and directions, stash the pages in my laptop bag, and get ready for bed. Another day trip, another twenty-five hundred U.S., I keep repeating to myself. Like an extremely bad example of a Buddhist mantra.

The departure sign at the airport says my flight leaves from gate 63. I have never heard of gate 63. Perhaps it's next to platform 9 3/4, because it certainly feels like I've entered another dimension as I walk down an endless nondescript corridor I hope will take me to my conveyance to Raleigh. I go upstairs and downstairs and upstairs again. When I get there, the waiting room for gate 63 is devoid of humans. There isn't even anyone at the check-in counter. I look up at the monitor that displays flights and am relieved to see a plane to Raleigh is supposed to leave at eight forty-five. And that Hogwarts is not on the board.

It's only seven o'clock, so I dump my laptop bag on a row of delightful orange-coloured molded fibreglass chairs and wait for someone to show up. And wait. And wait. It's now approaching eight o'clock. According to Robin, this is my one and only chance to get to Raleigh today.

There's a bank of payphones near the stairs. I spend a few minutes debating whether or not I should call him. I know that reaching him is about as unlikely as finding out I'm actually on my way to wizard school. But if I leave a message, at least I'll be on the record as having tried if I miss the plane.

I'm not surprised that the phone rings and rings until Robin's message kicks in. *Robin here! I'm on another call! Leave your number and I'll get back to you ASAP! Happy travels!* He can't possibly be on another call. He never answers the phone.

After the beep, I'm as politely succinct as possible under the circumstances. "Robin, it's me. I don't know why the Raleigh flight isn't at this gate. What should I do? I'm at a payphone at Terminal 1. The number is 416-555-7300. Please call me back. I'm frantic." And I'm not kidding. There's sweat trickling down the inside of the arms of my suit jacket. After the sauna weather of the other Henderson, I have no idea why I thought this outfit would be a good idea. Too late now. On the plus side, if I have to do this again tomorrow, my future self will thank me for the wardrobe advice.

I return to the supremely uncomfortable Siamese quadruplet chairs and sit back down. Then get back up again. I think better on my feet. I don't know if I have the number for the place I'm visiting in North Carolina. But I realize that doesn't matter. All I'd need to do is call Holly. And leave a message. And hope she gets it in time to tell them I'll be there tomorrow instead. If that's even possible. I run through all the potential scenarios: the client's happy to reschedule, the client's pissed off and will never speak to us again, the client is busy until a month from now. Simon fires me.

But if I've learned even one lesson in my travels so far, not much is actually under my control. A welcome epiphany. I'm pretty sure it could have taken many years of therapy to reach this level of insight. And all it took was a couple of months in airports. I sit down and watch the clock ticking relentlessly toward eight forty-five. *Ommm* says my inside voice. Unconvincingly.

Suddenly, an Air Canada employee bustles through. He sees me and looks startled. "Are you waiting for the Raleigh flight? You should be at the terminal by now." I tell him I thought I was at the terminal.

"No! No! No! The Jazz flights leave from the satellite terminal. You have to get here an hour in advance for the shuttle bus. We can only run the buses at certain times of the day because they have to cross the taxiway." I guess I've perfected my pathetic look, because he gets on his walkie-talkie. From what I can make out from the static, he's trying to find someone to take me to the plane. He carries on an unintelligible conversation for a few minutes until he finally raises his fist in triumph.

"You're in luck! There's some weather in Raleigh. Takeoff's delayed for at least half an hour. Follow me to the shuttle." He ushers me down a flight of stairs to a set of sliding doors, where there's a bus parked at the curb.

In the distance, I hear the payphone ringing. Sweat, Robin. Sweat.

46

Evidently, the rule for being a town named Henderson is to have exactly the same topography and economy. Pancakes would lose the contest for flatness against the endless fields of tobacco and cotton I pass on my route to my North Carolina destination. When I finally reach the town, I find a Hallmark movie set, complete with ample Stars and Stripes flying over the doors of the main street's white siding-clad stores and angle parking spots populated with dad cars and pickup trucks. As there should be, there's the requisite white courthouse with a clock tower.

Despite the flight delay, I'm a little ahead of schedule, so I tour the sleepy residential side streets. Porches appear to be mandatory, as are manicured lawns and black-faced jockeys holding up mailboxes. I have time to grab lunch before my one thirty meeting, so I continue down the sedate avenues in search of a diner.

I find Alice's Restaurant in a gas station. There are still pumps outside, but they look too old to possibly still be in use. I surprise myself as I slide flawlessly into an angle parking spot at the curb. I'll need to report this to Fred. I wish I could take a picture. Not as hard as parallel parking, which we have not yet attempted, but tricky enough in my opinion.

When I enter the restaurant, I head to a stool at the counter. It's that kind of place. The waitress's nametag says

Bertha, not Alice. She's sporting classic diner attire: a blue puffed-sleeve dress and a white apron. Her pencil is firmly situated behind her ear and a coffee pot is probably permanently attached to her left hand.

"Don't think you're from these parts," she says. "What can I getcha, hun? Got us some hot roast beef sandwiches and banquet burgers and if you're extra hungry, ribs are on the go."

I glance at the menu. Definitely meat-forward. But it's a diner. They must have breakfast. Even for lunch. "Can I have a cheese omelette? With home fries?"

"Don't got home fries, whatever they are. Want grits?" When I decline her offer, she looks askance.

"And a tea," I add.

I look around the diner as I wait for my lunch. It has the typical décor of booths, Formica counters, and vinyl floors. Black and white tiles where the white has become almost indistinguishable from the black. People happily chowing down on plates heaped with charred meat with pitchers of iced tea on the table. I also notice I'm the only white person in the place. A very, very, white person. With red hair. But nobody seems concerned about this.

My lunch arrives. An omelette with cheese but also infested with sausage. A glass of iced tea instead of a hot beverage. And what must be grits: a pile of yellowish mush with the consistency of wallpaper paste. I push the food around and rearrange it to look like I might have eaten some of it. I pay my tab and leave a tip Simon would probably not approve of.

The M.R. Williams company, my destination, has a huge confederate flag flying in front of the building and a prominent sign on the front door that says *No concealed weapons*. I'm a little confused about this. Does that mean if enter in full Lara Croft mode, I'm okay? I'm not sure I even want to know the answer to that.

When I open the door, the receptionist greets me effusively. "Hi. Welcome. Mike's waiting for you in the conference room. Hope you had a good trip here." I'm thankful she doesn't ask about my guns. Or more importantly, lack of guns.

I do my usual small talk to get the interview started. "Had a great lunch at Alice's Restaurant," I say. "Remember that song by Arlo Guthrie? Kind of a cute name."

"You went over the tracks? To the coloured side?" he seems horrified.

I don't remember crossing any tracks. Maybe he's being metaphorical? Maybe not. "Well, I was just looking for lunch. Didn't know what was good in town. Lunch was very good."

"Heard there's some tasty food there," he says. "They musta thought you didn't know white folks don't belong. What with that red hair and all." I nod and smile. My new benign face. I ask him to tell me about his company.

Mike tells me he started his company, M.R. Williams, back in the mid seventies, when he noticed how much traffic went in and out of his local 7-Eleven and realized how much profit margin there must be in impulse purchases at corner stores and gas stations. "We supply just about everything convenience stores need. Tobacco. Confections. Phone cards. Heck, we even supply the tuck shops at the jails and you gotta know we got lots of jails here in Carolina. Virginia too!

"But let me tell you how our business succeeds. Upwards of seventy percent of convenience store purchases are spontaneous. If you have the right high-profit stuff in the right place you can rake the bucks in. We've also designed this thing we call 'novelty express.' It's a bunch of stuff that we guarantee will maximize corner store profitability. Chips, candy, cigarettes. All the major food groups.

"The other thing we're very proud of is getting the government to allow convenience stores to accept food stamps. What could be better than making it easier for families to buy nutritious meals close to home?" I don't ask him what could possibly be nutritious about dubious heat-lamp hot dogs, chips, candy, and cigarettes.

"Inventory management is the thing. It's all about volume and turnover. But only 10% of the stores we supply were automated. And none of the prisons. Now with our ASP, we offer a free online inventory order and management portal. Bob's your uncle. If they stop ordering, we can fire them. If they're low on Mars bars, we can top them up within hours. And we can drop-ship cigarettes to the jails in bulk. It's a licence to print money!"

The slime I'll need to scrape from my skin after this interview even tops Sunshine Savings and Loan. How I'm going to pull a falcon out of this one escapes me at the moment. And maybe forever.

47

"What do you think about the Bruce Cockburn thing?" says Fred. Today we're doing the southern east–west highway. It's relatively easy because it has fewer lanes than the northern one, and fewer lanes mean it's more congested and more congested means it moves slower and moving slower means I don't need to go very fast.

"I was here on the weekend. I know all about it. It's about time he got into the Canadian Music Hall of Fame. He's been able to move beyond the folky stuff to top ten radio. By the way, Fred, I've figured out what you're doing. You don't care about Bruce Cockburn. Or the Dionne quintuplets. You're just trying to distract me from my inside voice. The one that I'm always trying to convince not to kill me in a car accident." Contrary to my fully functioning adult self, my inside voice does not seem to want me to drive.

"You got me," says Fred. "But it's workin'." I tell him he's right and that clearly I've done enough driving lessons. I'm finished here. "If you say so, grasshopper." But somehow I don't think he really thinks I'm ready.

***

Holly's inhabiting her usual spot on my answering machine when I get home.

Hi! It's Holly! You are going to beautiful Pittsburgh. To see how the sausage is made. Haha! Johnsonville Sausage is your destination. Maybe they'll give you some to take home. These guys don't actually sound weird.

Beep.

Robin here. Pittsburgh's a direct hop. Your car will be at Fastbreak as usual. You're racking up those Budget points!

I can't imagine what I'll do with Budget points because I can't imagine renting a car for fun. Maybe I can gift them to Simon. Or Holly.

I print my usual MapQuest map, then, just for fun, root around the internet for information on Pittsburgh. Wikipedia says its nickname is the "city of bridges" because there are 446 of them in the vicinity. Uh-oh. I'm not good with bridges. It says the city is at the confluence of the Allegheny and Monongahela Rivers, which combine to form the Ohio River. I need to remember that for trivia. Evidently, all roads lead to the Ohio River. All of my roads, anyhow.

As promised, there's my name on the Fastbreak board. It's a red Honda Civic this time. With Kentucky plates. I guess by now I've spent enough time in Kentucky to make this completely appropriate. I carefully review my MapQuest directions. The route looks straightforward: I-376 east to the Fort Pitt Tunnel that'll take me to the Fort Pitt Bridge that'll take me over the Monongahela River to downtown Pittsburgh. Easy peasy.

The Fort Pitt Tunnel is exactly that. A tunnel. I have no choice but to literally go with the flow of the I-376 into the horizontal abyss. It's tube shaped, which is probably what a tunnel should look like. I was picturing a dark cocoon, like what you see in movies when trains go through tunnels. Thank goodness, it's lit up like a Las Vegas night. There are three lanes that go in the same direction, and I stick to my method of clinging to the right because that's where the exits always are. The other direction must be through another tunnel. I tell my thoughts of *what would happen if there was an accident and how would ambulances possibly get here and would you even be able to call 9-1-1 from here* to mind their own business.

Once I get the hang of it, the drive is actually pretty manageable. Like a carnival ride that moves along on a fixed track, pretending it's putting you in peril but impossible to derail. After about a mile, I can see light at the end of the tunnel. Ha! Can't wait to tell Fred that one. I congratulate myself profusely on traversing my first-ever tunnel, which exits onto the Fort Pitt Bridge and will hopefully funnel me directly to my destination in downtown Pittsburgh. There's another one for Fred. A tunnel funnel! These thoughts only momentarily distract me from another thing.

There are no bridges in Toronto. Fred never taught me how to drive over bridges. He probably thought bridges were no-brainers. My brain certainly thinks it should be involved. Heights and I don't get along. I've tried many times to improve the relationship, but I've always ended up doing all the work. Heights just never budge. They insist on remaining high. The Fort Pitt Bridge is no different.

A travel writer would probably be effusive about the "panoramic view of Pittsburgh's skyline" afforded by the upper level of the inbound bridge, which also has three one-way lanes. Not me. But I have no choice but to keep my eyes on the road as I "admire" the view, hands clenched on the steering wheel. Hyperventilating and writing my obituary in my head.

I'm happy to finally see some exit signs up ahead. I will probably live to see the end of this bridge. *Downtown Pittsburgh. Exit left. 300 feet.* Exit left? Fred never told me it was possible to exit on the left. The cars in the lanes beside me are bumper to bumper. If I could even will my hands to put on a turn signal, there's no way I'd be able to get across the traffic in time.

I keep to my lane as the bridge ends and find myself under an overpass somewhere that looks a little dodgy. The sooty steel girders of the overpass are covered in semi-literate graffiti that mostly involves things people's mothers are purported to have done. There are massive piles of garbage near the curbs. The overpass is obstructing the light so it looks like the end of the day, instead of an hour before lunch. I can't let Fred down, but I'm not going anywhere unless I can start breathing properly. I manage to pilot the car into the lot of what looks like it used to be a convenience store. It's boarded up and decorated with more unimaginative graffiti.

There's also a phone booth. I sit in the car for about twenty minutes, trying to regulate my heart rate. I look more closely at the phone booth. The cord of the receiver dangles, without benefit of mouthpiece. I don't have a phone number to call, anyhow. Or anybody to help me. Except me. The only person who can help me is me.

I take stock of my surroundings again. There's a Citgo gas station sign a few blocks away. Aren't you supposed to ask for directions at gas stations? I start the car and get back on the street.

48

The front door of the gas station store is clad in iron bars. A sign on the door says to look up into the closed-circuit camera before pressing the buzzer. I guess I don't seem threatening, because the door opens. The clerk is behind a Plexiglas cage that goes from the counter up to the ceiling. I approach him slowly, trying to look as innocuous as possible. I slide my crumpled MapQuest instructions under a slot. "Do you know how I'd get there from here? I'm really lost."

"You sure are," says the attendant as he puzzles over my crumpled printout. "You're a ways away from there. And wouldn't be so smart to hang around these parts any longer than you need to. What company did you say you're going to?"

"Johnsonville. The sausage people."

"Oh! I know them. They have a huge sign with a sausage on top. You can see it from the overpass." I tell him I need to get there without any involvement from overpasses. He nods, takes a well-chewed pencil out of his shirt pocket, and marks a circuitous route on my map. "This should do it," he says. "Do me a favour and follow it exactly. Don't even think about deviating from this route. May the Lord guide your journey." I nod solemnly. And go with his God.

And indeed, his directions, or maybe his God, work. I arrive at the sausage factory a scant two hours after I was supposed to be there. I park in an ample lot and cross my fingers.

"Thank goodness you're here," says the receptionist. "We were worried you'd gotten lost. Ben's been holding all calls. He's been so excited for the meeting. He'll be down in a few minutes." I uncross my fingers. And unclench my jaw.

"We'll start with a factory tour, if you want," says Ben, who's clad in what I assume is Pittsburgh splendor. Khaki pants. Black running shoes. Polo shirt with a Johnsonville logo. I'm tempted to repeat Holly's joke about getting to see how the sausages are made, but I don't. I tell Ben that would be great.

We don lab coats and hairnets and paper booties that look like shower caps over our shoes. Neither my hair nor my shoes are happy with this. Ben also hands me a yellow hard hat that says VIP and has an embossed label with my name on it. "You can even keep the hard hat," he says, proving he was indeed extremely excited about this interview. I'm a little concerned about the hard hat. Could there be pigs falling from the sky? Or, heaven forbid, pig parts?

Next, he gives me some ear protectors that look like headphones. It takes me a few minutes to figure out if they go over or under the hard hat. I opt for over. A very elegant fashion statement to say the least. "Pretty loud in here," he says. And so far, very low tech. Meat grinders. Belts conveying ground meat. Sausage casings getting stuffed with pork. I'm actually enjoying seeing sausages being made but can't yet figure out how an ASP factors into this. Nor can I figure out how I'm going to explain I don't want to keep the hard hat.

Back in a conference room, having now divested myself of my protective equipment, Ben fills me in. Johnsonville has entered the twenty-first century via a website. "People exchange sausage recipes and have fun!" He manages to talk about Johnsonville.com and the excitement of going online for two hours, as I scribble frantically. When he pauses to take a drink of water, I ask him if they also sell the sausages online.

"Yes! We get almost two orders a day!" Not exactly the pinnacle of e-commerce, but I think I'll be able to manufacture my own sausage out of this. I thank him for his hospitality when it appears we're done.

"The internet's definitely changing how businesses work," I say. "You're on the grunting edge!"

"Wow. Can I use that?"

"Yup," I say. Me too. Falcon material!

We walk out past what looks like a store. "This is our company store. The bricks and mortar version," says Ben. "All employees can shop here whenever they want. Hey, why not take some home with you?" I want to say no, but Ben is so enthusiastic, I let him put packs of frozen bratwurst and spicy Italian links in an insulated bag. I'm under the twenty-four hours again. And is meat even allowed across the border? He also gives me a Johnsonville fridge magnet. Shaped like a sausage, of course. Maybe the best magnet yet.

I thank him again and head out to my car. I stash my stuff in the back seat, put on my seat belt, check the mirror positioning like Fred says, when I see Ben in the rear-view mirror, running toward the car. He's brandishing the yellow hard hat. "You forgot this," he says. I crank down the window and reach out to grab the reluctant souvenir. He lifts his right hand to salute me. "This case study is going to make my career!" I'm hoping it makes mine too, Ben, my inside voice replies. If I manage to make it home.

I consult my reverse MapQuest directions. There doesn't seem to be any way, save learning to beam myself there, to get to the airport without doing the bridge and tunnel again. Maybe my hard hat will come in handy. I briefly consider putting it on, then I give my head a shake. I take a deep breath, which I'm expecting might have to last me for some time, and aim the car in the direction of the bridge.

49

Apparently, my lizard brain still prefers that I survive, because I manage to make it across the bridge and through to the end of the tunnel. I exhale, not realizing I hadn't breathed in a while. I manage to get to the rental car drop-off without further incident, retrieve my sausage care package and hard hat and walk toward the terminal's departure gates.

When we're on our descent into Toronto, it occurs to me that sausages are not jeans. I can't claim they play any kind of role in travelling light. Even a deviant one. I flip over the customs form. "Do you have any meat or meat products?" it asks.

In the arrival hall, there's a customs agent with a cute little beagle on a leash, leading the dog through the hall to sniff at carry-on luggage. He may be looking for contraband drugs, but what canine can resist partially thawed meat?

I look back at the door where I came in and notice that near the entrance to the arrival hall, there's a bathroom. I saunter casually to the ladies' sanctuary, trying my best to deflect attention from my insulated bag that says Johnsonville Sausages in bright red letters on the side. Reluctantly, I cram the whole thing into the garbage receptacle underneath the paper towel dispenser. I hope I don't smell like sausage.

The hard hat is still in my clutches as the customs agent waves me through without question. Thankfully he seems to think it's normal for a woman wearing a business suit to be carrying a yellow head protector with her name on it. Just another Thursday night. It's then I remember my sausage fridge magnet was in the bag with the sausages.

***

"What do you think about the Conrad Black thing?" Fred launches into his usual driving chit-chat on Friday.

"Come on Fred, do we have to keep doing this? It's bad enough I had to come crawling back for more lessons. He's mad at Canada and is going to live in England. They know all about it south of the border. He's got lots of friends down there. I think he even has a house in Florida."

"Okay. I'll cut it out. But it's not my fault there aren't any tunnels or bridges around here. Unless you want to drive out all the way to the Burlington Skyway. That's sort of bridge-like."

"No, let's forget about bridges. I only have a few trips left. I'll just do a bit more research before I go anywhere and plan routes to avoid bridges if I can."

I've finally realized it's going to be impossible to anticipate situations that might throw me into a spin, with or without the car spinning as well. Accept the things we cannot change and all that serenity stuff that I've yet to master. When Fred drops me off, I'm noncommittal about booking another date. Won't be long before I can hang up my driving gloves for good, if I had driving gloves.

The flashing light beckons when I get home. Gotta be Holly or Robin. But no, it's Simon.

I guess you're on the road. We're closing in on the end of this thing. Well, not really the end because we still have to pull the report together, but the interviews should all be wrapped up in two weeks. Robin's working on getting you to Orlando the week after next, but there'll be one more before that. Holly's got something near Nashville. Anyhow, good work so far.

Beep.

Hi! It's Holly! Hope you like the Grand Ole Opry and own a pair of cowboy boots! I'm still finalizing the timing, but there's a hospital near Nashville that's been recommended by IBM. Sounds a little bizarre but that's not my problem! More details to come.

I'm pretty sure Nashville's inland. There couldn't possibly be bridges involved. Could there?

50

The U.S. immigration line snakes back and forth as usual, corralling us with those fat red ribbon-like dividers that are attached to three-foot-high posts. We're not moving very quickly today, which is actually more annoying than not moving at all. Every five minutes or so, I need to pick up my stuff, carry it a foot, then put it back down. After I do this for about the tenth time, I'm adjacent to a guy who looks familiar.

"Hi," he says. "Where are you off to today?" I guess I look familiar to him, too. Unless he's just unusually friendly. But that's not likely. Friendly is a characteristic that is diametrically opposed to travel self-preservation, where survival depends on looking out for oneself at all costs.

I run my brain through my face rolodex, cross-referencing against employers and clients, and filtering by potential venues, locales, and geographic coordinates. Nothing. But the line's not going anywhere, and it'll be a while before they call me out of the pack to race to my flight. "Nashville," I say.

"I've seen you here every week," he says. "The red hair. Plus there aren't many road warrior girls. Are you always going to Nashville?"

I have kind of noticed that the people I see in the cross-border lineup all look vaguely familiar, but I just thought that's because all the guys look the same: same backpacks, same pair of Levi's, same brown slip-on shoes, same navy blue suit jacket, same open-necked blue dress shirt, same garment bag, which presumably holds the suit pants and some additional shirts.

I tell him I go somewhere different each time.

"Wow! That's a real slog. Different hotel every time. Different airport every time. Different route to get where you're going. Hey, are you signed up for the SeatGuru newsletter and the points optimizer tip sheet that dude Rocco puts out?" I shake my head.

"I'll show you mine if you show me yours," he says. I look around the crowded customs hall. I have no idea what he's talking about. I'm certainly not showing him anything. Even my boarding pass. He could be a serial killer who'll show up at my Nashville hotel.

He pulls his out of his wallet and unfolds an accordion of embossed plastic, holding loyalty cards. He has all the major hotel chains and rental car brands and most of the airlines.

"Why so many?" Oops. Maybe that's a question an amateur traveller might ask. That's bound to muck up my status, the security guy in Henderson notwithstanding.

"Well, it's all about playing them off each other. When I go to Hertz, I make sure they notice I have the Budget and Avis cards as well. If they don't automatically offer me an upgrade, I say that Avis always gives me one, then I look over at the Avis counter and pretend I'm getting ready to go across the aisle. If you know anything about computer stuff, you'll know their system tells them exactly how many times I've rented a car in the past months, which is a heck of a lot. Same for the hotels, although it's a little more complicated. Works best if you're travelling with a buddy. Our modus operandi — that's Latin, by the way — is when we're waiting to check in, to talk loudly about all the great perks we're getting from some other chain. When we get to the counter, I've usually scored a suite and a free breakfast. I've heard that for girls, it always works if you look pathetic."

Paging flight 537 to Nashville. All passengers please proceed to counter number 5.

"That's me," I say. "Thanks for the tips." And now that I only have two trips left, there's barely any time to see if they work. I guess I still have more to learn about travelling.

I arrive in Nashville on time and without incident. I make my way down a typical nondescript beige corridor that could be in any airport in North America, except there's no doubt I'm in Music City because they're piping in some raucous country tunes. I pass through the departure lounge for the gate where we arrived and follow the signs to ground transportation. The music's getting louder and louder. Then I see there's a low stage set up near the windows. A five-piece band with full amplification, illuminated by blue floodlights, decked out in satin Western shirts and ten-gallon cowboy hats, is singing "Boot Scootin' Boogie." And it's barely noon.

A small crowd has gathered around, and an open guitar case displays a substantial mound of U.S. cash. I'm liking Nashville so far. Anything that can make the airport experience less soul-sucking is fine with me, even if the choice of repertoire isn't exactly family-friendly.

I continue to the rental car area and walk to the Fastbreak sign. Then I stop. There's plenty of time to spare since I have nowhere to be except my hotel. The Avis counter has no lineup.

"Can I sign up for Preferred here?" Yes, indeed I can, according to the guy manning the desk. He asks for my identifying coordinates, punches the information into his terminal, and hands me a card made of paper.

"They'll mail you the official one," he says. "But you can start earning points right away." I thank him and go back to the Budget counter.

"That's me on the Fastbreak board," I say. "What car do I have?" The clerk shuffles some papers and tells me I have Toyota Camry. "What have you got that's one level up? Maybe a convertible?"

He pecks at his terminal. "I have a Mustang two-door. Red. Ragtop. The upgrade would be an extra thirty dollars a day."

"Hmm. Avis will give me one for the cost of the Toyota."

Just like the guy in Toronto said would happen, he frowns, abuses his keyboard some more, then picks up the phone. "So Phil, this lady has rented from us every week for the past two months. Full freight. She eligible for a level two?" He listens for a minute, then resumes his version of typing. "Row 1. Number 5. Keys are in the ignition. Paperwork's in the glovebox. Just sign here and you're good to go. Thank you for choosing Budget."

51

Just one problem. I've never driven a convertible. Or a sports car. Are they different than regular cars? Another thing Fred never mentioned, but I hear his voice in my head as I get into the Mustang. *Adjust the seat. Check the mirrors. Review the dashboard controls.*

The dashboard controls look like they were cloned from the bridge on the International Space Station. There are multiple LED displays and various levers and buttons. I wouldn't be surprised if one of them deploys a Canadarm that'll emerge from the nether regions of the trunk. I turn on the ignition, which thankfully uses a key, like normal. The shift control is on the console between the driver's and passenger seats, like normal. If I just stick with the things that look normal, it'll be okay.

But there's no obvious way to put the top down or up. What would happen if it rains and I can't get it to go back up? What if somehow the roof got wrecked and I'm on the hook for the damage? What was I thinking asking for a convertible? Will my inside voice ever shut up?

I consult my MapQuest printout, which I hadn't reviewed in detail before now. Seems like it's a pretty straight run from here to my downtown hotel. Then I look a little closer. There's a river to cross. Is there any city or town in the U.S. that isn't on a body of water that must be forded in some manner? I think not. Phantom Fred pipes up again. *Don't wimp out. Stop being an idiot. You're the boss.*

I'm relieved to discover that, as far as bridges go, Nashville's are barely worthy of acrophobia. Besides the one I'm on, there are a handful of them that span the Cumberland River at random intervals, all of them barely hovering above the narrow waterway. Add that to my low-slung sporty chassis and I can't see anything other than the steel railing. And that's a good thing.

Downtown Nashville has the requisite main boulevard that leads to a white courthouse with a clock tower. There's also a main commercial drag with low-rise storefronts and chain restaurants and a complete lack of residential structures since only tourists would dare venture downtown after the sidewalks roll up.

"Valet or self-park?" the attendant asks me when I arrive at the hotel. I'm guessing valet is more expensive so I'll bet Simon would not approve.

"Self-park," I say, with an assured frequent traveller tone of voice that comes out of my mouth with no involvement from me.

"Go out the driveway and turn left on the street behind us. You'll see the parking garage entrance."

A parking garage. Right. Of course. Yet another gaping hole in my driving education. All the hotels I've had to park at so far have had vast outdoor lots. But I insisted on staying downtown. With an expensive convertible that might get dinged. Or stolen. Don't they steal cars from underground garages? I think they also murder people in them. At least they do in American TV shows, so that must be true.

The street behind the hotel is narrow and one-way. It's flanked by three-storey buildings, many of which are boarded up and covered in graffiti tags. The garage door lifts slowly as I nose the car onto the pitch-dark ramp that leads down to the parking spots. I drive up to the barrier that's across the entrance, then have to jam on the brakes when it stays stubbornly in place. Maybe the hotel needs to know my licence plate number first. I back up and circle back around to the hotel.

"Valet or self-park?" the attendant says. They must get a lot of red Mustang convertibles here. He seems to have no recollection that I was just here five minutes ago.

"Self-park," I say, without the self-assured frequent traveller voice, which has decided to abandon me in my hour of need. "But how does it work? Do I need to check in to the hotel first?"

"Nope, just go out the driveway and turn left on the street behind us. You'll see the parking garage entrance. Take the ticket from the machine. But don't leave it in your car. Don't want anyone to steal it for the price of a day's parking." See? I was right. They do steal cars from the garage!

I retrace my route to the garage door, which rises even slower than last time, if that was even possible. Once again, I approach the barrier. Once again, I'm flummoxed. Ticket? What ticket? I roll down the window to improve my view through the gloom but don't see any place to grab a ticket. *Breathe.* I lean back into the headrest and do as Fred instructs. Then I see it. There's a ticket machine on the left. Only it's above the roof of my car. Perfect height if you're in a pickup truck. And I oughta know about that. I get out of my ridiculous convertible and reach up to take the ticket. The barrier rises as it should.

The ramp winds down and down to what I'm sure is just a smidgen above the Cumberland River's water table. I find a spot I decide is the least likely to attract carjackers. Over near the elevator where at least there's a dim white bulb on the ceiling, encased in a metal cage, and some ambient light from an exit sign that's strobing on and off. Mostly off. My nascent regret for both the redness and potential toplessness of my ride has now become a bottomless chasm of contrition.

52

The Nashville hotel concierge is appalled. "You want to eat somewhere other than here? And you want to walk there?" I've decided I deserve to take myself out, since I'm almost finished my road trips and I'm explaining I want a restaurant recommendation. Somewhere close. I have no desire to navigate the parking garage more times than I need to, but I do have a desire for a fancy meal.

In my now extensive experience, hotel dining rooms aim their sights firmly on the lowest common denominator of culinary tastes, while pretending to be refined. A Wagyu beef burger. Chicken Kiev. Spaghetti al pomodoro. In other words, an expensive hamburger, an expensive chicken breast, and an expensive plate of pasta.

The concierge spends the next five minutes trying to convince me that the fabulous restaurant in this very hotel is the best place to eat for miles. "Our chef does wonders with Wagyu beef! We have the best chicken Kiev in town! And our pasta! You couldn't get a better spaghetti in Rome!" He clearly thinks I'm a garden-variety tourist, instead of a member of three frequent flyer clubs and now holder of a six-inch-high stack of loyalty cards. And I'm guessing he gets a cut of the tips.

I listen politely. Then I say, "Thanks for your help. I'll just walk out and see what I can find." The concierge looks at me like I've told him I'm going to run naked across the stage of the Grand Ole Opry. I remain standing in front of the desk for another moment, then head to the revolving doors that lead to the street.

"Ma'am! Ma'am! There is a steakhouse that's not far. Hy's. I can call them for you." I congratulate myself on having perfected my steely resolve expression and walk back to the concierge's post. "It should take you ten minutes at most to get there. I'll call them now and tell them to expect you at 6:45. When you get there, tell them to call me back to say you've arrived. If I don't hear from them, I'll send the police to look for you." Seems a little drastic to me, but if that's what he wants to do, I'll play along if it results in a decent place to eat.

I have my laptop bag with me, but without the laptop. I thought I'd bring my notebook so I have something to do while I wait for my dinner. I turn left as I exit the hotel and follow the instructions to get to the steakhouse. It's pretty straightforward. A few blocks along the same street as the hotel and then a right turn onto the street where the restaurant is.

I'm halfway to my right turn when I see two police officers coming my way. Surely the concierge didn't report me missing yet. I continue on my journey, getting closer to the cops. They're looking directly at me. "Ma'am," one of them says. "Where are you going? Why are you out walking?" I chortle at the story I can tell Fred about how it's illegal not to drive in Nashville.

"To Hy's," I say. "For dinner. It's just around the corner."

"Come with us. We'll escort you," he says. I guess that's how they do things here, so I let them lead me the two more blocks to the restaurant. They walk me inside to the maître d's podium.

"Can you please call the Marriott's concierge and tell him I've arrived?" I say. The policemen nod approvingly.

"We walk this route until midnight. We pass here at ten after the hour. Wait for us when you're ready to go back to the hotel." I promise them that's what I'll do. I don't want to get arrested for disobeying the police.

A hostess escorts me through a room that's as dark as a crypt. What little décor I can see through the dim light features lots of flocked wallpaper and mahogany panelling. So much for reviewing my notes. It would be impossible to see the pages.

When I'm seated on a red velvet banquette, I place my laptop bag near my feet, propped up on the legs of the chair on the other side of the table. A waiter hands me a huge gold-tasselled menu and a tiny flashlight and recites the specials of the day. He takes my drink request and retreats while I peruse the food on offer. It will definitely beat any hotel dining room. I decide on the whole red snapper.

The waiter brings my glass of chardonnay and nods approvingly at my choice of fish. There's nothing left to do but try to eavesdrop or make up stories about my fellow diners. There are several older men who've been kind enough to treat their daughters to a steak dinner, but they're too far away for me to hear any conversation. The gents are very funny, though, based on how loudly the women are laughing.

The waiter returns with a trolley, where a half-dozen snappers are splayed out on a bed of ice. At least I didn't have to catch my own dinner, but it appears audience participation is required. I point to the specimen in the middle and receive another appreciative head-bowing from the waiter. While I sip my wine, I amuse myself by revisiting the tales I can tell my NTN team when I get back. They'll think I'm making it up.

My snapper arrives on a platter the size of a football field, adorned with sprigs of parsley but nothing else. "Was this supposed to come with vegetables?" I ask the waiter.

"All the sides are à la carte," he says. "That's French for not included, or something like that. There's the baked potato at twenty dollars. Creamed spinach at twenty-two dollars. Or peas and carrots, at twenty-four ninety-five." For that price, they must back a truck full of vegetables to the table. I tell the waiter it's just fine as is.

I manage to make it through about a quarter of my fish before I give up. When the waiter whisks the mangled snapper away, I decline a doggy bag and request the bill. He gives me a puzzled look. I guess he didn't hear me. "Just the bill," I say.

"Oh," he says. "You mean the check."

Right. It's the *check* here. I never remember that. I reach down to retrieve my laptop bag, pick it up the wrong way and a bunch of things fall out. It's too dark to see exactly what, but I reach around under the table and put what I find back in the bag. My police escort will be arriving in the 'hood in five minutes.

53

When I get to my hotel room door, I go through my bag to find my keycard. Which isn't there. I root around in the front pocket. Still no card. I fan the pages of my notebook. Nothing. I even check inside my wallet, in case I put it away in there. No dice. Then it dawns on me. It's probably languishing in Hy's gloom.

I've never lost my keycard before. I guess they can replace it. I go down to the front desk and tell them what happened. It only takes her a few seconds to manufacture a new card and slide it to me over the counter. She does not ask me for ID. "It's probably under a table at Hy's," I say. "Should I be worried about that?"

The clerk tells me she'll let security know. "You need a keycard to get into the hotel after nine. If the guards see anyone trying to get in who they don't recognize, they'll deal with it." I say I'm leaving early in the morning for the airport, so I won't be in the room very long anyhow.

My flight is at eight o'clock, which means I'll need to be out of here by five-thirty, which means I'll need to be up by four thirty, which means I can get six hours sleep if I start now. Better not to risk getting my shut-eye interrupted. I prop the desk chair under the doorknob, just like they do in the movies.

The alarm goes off as scheduled and I congratulate myself for having had a quasi-restful night. After a quick shower, I pack up my stuff and go down to check out. There's a tray of muffins and croissants on a sideboard in the lobby and urns filled with coffee and hot water. I grab a carrot muffin and make myself a tea to go. I get a free breakfast and I'll be home by lunchtime. I can pocket twenty-five bucks. U.S.

I take the elevator down to P2. Everything has been going so well that I'm a little apprehensive about what condition the car will be in, if it hasn't been stolen. But there it is, still in pristine shape. It occurs to me I probably should have gotten the keys out before I came down to the deserted parking lot — the concierge would be apoplectic — but the place seems deserted so I'm not freaked out as I reach in to retrieve them from the zippered part of my laptop bag. Except they aren't there. Nor are they in the front flap. Or in my suit jacket pocket. I'm pretty sure they're relaxing under my table at Hy's, keeping the keycard company. The restaurant doesn't open until noon.

I could miss my flight, go back to the hotel, wait until Hy's opens, and go get the keys, but that would entail phoning Robin, getting his voicemail and having to explain on tape what happened. And I may or may not be able to get on another flight.

Then my road warrior persona kicks in. *Just leave the car where it is, catch a cab to the airport, and practise your pathetic expression for the rental car people.* And hope I don't get the same clerk.

The cab to the airport takes the ramp to departures. "No, no! I need to go to arrivals!" The driver looks puzzled but takes a long loop around the terminal as the meter ticks away. This is going to eat my breakfast and lunch money. I just hope I don't also have to pay to replace a Mustang convertible. I get the driver to drop me at the arrivals-level ground transportation door.

There's a woman at the Budget desk. I'm not sure if that's good or bad. I'm not sure how to play this. Ditzy woman travelling alone in a strange city? Naïve woman travelling in a foreign land? Businesswoman with authority who doesn't need to make excuses? I opt for the latter. I can hear Fred applauding.

"Excuse me," I say. "There's an issue with my rental return."

"I'm so sorry," she says. "What can I do to fix it?"

"The car is in the parking garage at the Marriott downtown. This is the parking lot ticket. Someone will need to go and retrieve it. The cost of parking will be put on my hotel account when they exit the garage."

"Oh! Was there a problem with the car?"

"Yes. It wouldn't start. I had to take a cab here to make sure I could make my flight out of the country. If I miss it, I'll be stuck here for another day."

"I'm so sorry, Ma'am. We'll take care of it. And we'll reverse the charges for the rental. Thank you for choosing Budget and again I'm sorry for the inconvenience."

I'm smart enough to wait until I get to the departures area to do my happy dance. Nobody will ever be the wiser. Except Fred. And my NTN crew. And my hairdresser. And the guy from the immigration line.

This is just too good a story to keep to myself.

54

Orlando! says Simon on my machine. *It's going to be fantastic. So many interviews. And IBM throws a great conference. Last time they had Tina Turner as the entertainment. Everything's been arranged. Holly and Robin have the details.*

Beep.

Hi! It's Holly! Orlando! It's going to be fantastic. The happiest place on earth! Your itinerary's in your inbox. Your schedule is jam-packed. No sign of weirdos! Unless the IBM guys are weird. I've heard they can be.

Beep.

Robin here. Orlando! It's usually easy to get there, but flights are pretty busy this time of year since the kids are off school. No seats on Air Canada. Had to put you on WestJet. Terminal 3.

I'll worry about navigating Terminal 3 later. Right now, I need to get someone to look after the cat for four days. I walk down my porch stairs and up their Siamese twin to my neighbour's front door. Greg answers the bell, holding the section of the newspaper that has the crossword. "What's a six-letter word for 'corn product for grits'?"

"Hominy," I say triumphantly. "It's impossible to get breakfast without it in the U.S. At least in the parts I've been to. I'm headed out again. Four days this time. Ricky will need a sitter. Can you come over and feed him? Let him in and out periodically?"

Greg says he'd be happy to. "May even spend a bit of time at your place, too, if you don't mind. Judy isn't feeling well, and I think it's contagious. Pretty nasty. Requires spending a lot of time in the bathroom, if you get my drift." I tell him he can camp out as much as wants, as long as he cleans the cat dishes.

Greg follows me back to my side of the porch so I can show him Ricky's drill. "He won't eat the food if it's been sitting in the dish too long. He won't eat the food if it's been in the fridge. He won't eat the food if he's decided he doesn't like that flavour anymore. Other than that, he's pretty easy." I show him the litter bins. "I know he's just one cat, but he uses both bins. One for number one and one for number two. I'll write down the vet's number. I hope he won't need to go in, but if he does, be sure to ask for his 'frequent fighter discount.' I'll write down the number of the hotel where I'll be." I usher Greg out the door before he has a chance to change his mind. I have more important concerns than my cat. Like, what clothes am I going to pack for Orlando? And even more importantly, what shoes? For four days I'll definitely need a carry-on. Might as well fill it up.

Ricky, who's sleeping in the closet, complains at my intrusion on his personal space as I peruse my wall-mounted shoe rack. Clearly sandals are in order. But what colours and styles? A rainbow looks back at me. I have no idea what I might need. The blue suede slingbacks, I think. The pink slides. The funky green strappy numbers. The ridiculous Ralph Lauren heels in an adorably shimmery peach hue. In which I can stand at cocktail hour for exactly five minutes, without wanting to revert to barefoot. I doubt that Mr. Lauren has ever tried these suckers on. Much as is true about men designing cubicle workstations, men who make shoes have no idea about female anatomy.

***

Terminal 1 is the domain of Air Canada and its staid partners, Air France, KLM, and Lufthansa. Terminal 3 is the domain of the truly amateur traveller. Charter airlines. Cheap tickets. People who bring their entire extended family on fun-filled vacations to buffet-centric all-inclusive resorts in Cuba. Or to Disney World.

I'm out of place in my beige linen skirt suit, nude pantyhose, and red ballet flats, amid the throngs of Mickey Mouse t-shirts, capri pants, shorts, and flip-flops, wheeling strollers and failing mightily at corralling their snotty-nosed offspring in the direction of the security line. None of these people must have any idea what the microclimate is like on a plane at 30,000 feet. More akin to nuclear winter than a Florida beach.

I join the unruly crowd and try not to use my outside voice as I express my extreme dissatisfaction with my lot. I'm better than this! I'm not an amateur! Can't that woman tell her child to stop screaming? After about an hour, I finally make it to the front of the security line. I take out my laptop and put it in a bin. I take off my shoes and put them in another bin with my laptop bag and send it through the conveyer into the X-ray. I heft my carry-on up to the belt and do the same thing.

I look up at the departure board. I have about an hour until I need to be at my gate. Lots of time to grab a sandwich or salad for the plane. I've learned that this is important. I never know when I'll get a chance to eat.

My stuff starts to come back out of the X-ray tunnel. I grab the bin that holds my laptop bag and shoes. "Wait," says the security guy. "We need to swab your shoes. Shoe bomber guy and all that." He picks up my travel shoes, swabs them, puts the swab in some machine that's supposed to tell him if I'm a shoe bomber or not, and waits. After what seems like ten minutes, a green light goes off on the shoe bomber detector machine and he hands me back my shoes. I put them on and gather up the rest of my things.

"Wait," he says. "Do you have any other shoes?" I'm very tempted to say no. Then I review my options. Get arrested at the airport and miss my meetings in Orlando? Get my shoes confiscated?

"Yes. In my carry-on bag." He asks me to open my case and show him the five pairs of what I'm hoping are ideal, Orlando-appropriate shoes. He looks at me as if I've revealed I'm carrying a Volkswagen Beetle full of a hundred Shriners. He looks at the long line behind me. Then back at my shoes. Then takes his walkie-talkie out of the holster on his belt. In another interminable number of minutes, another security agent arrives.

"Brad here will take care of you," he says. Brad motions for me to move my carry-on to a stainless steel table on the other side of the security conveyor belt. He rolls up his sleeves as he prepares to start his monumental task. I watch the minutes accrue on the departure board clock as he removes each individual shoe with utmost care, applies his swab, and waits for the machine to tell him not to arrest me. Even though none of them could possibly harbour anything other than a bad pedicure. By the time he's finished certifying me as a non–shoe bomber, I have ten minutes to make my Orlando flight.

I dash through the concourse, find the gate and locate my seat on a plane packed full of squirming, whining children. I've just sat down when the pilot comes on with an announcement. I know by now that when the pilot speaks, one must listen. "Folks," he says, "we have a bit of a delay. Some stormy weather in Orlando. We'll need to wait until it clears. Appreciate your patience."

55

The slight delay has so far lasted three hours. Three sweltering hours. The best I can say is I'm in my customary exit row seat. Stomach rumbling. Crankiness quotient at DEFCON 2, where the next step is to deploy nuclear weapons. The wannabe Disney natives are extremely restless, expressing their displeasure with shrieks that would wake Beethoven, employing seatback kicks worthy of the UFC. There are also copious noxious smells I do not want to know the origin of. Several yards past the end of my rope, the pilot announces we're about to embark on our journey to the happiest place on earth. It had better be. The amount of happiness in this steel tube is way, way in the negative numbers.

The plane does make it to Orlando, and I congratulate myself on the dexterity with which I wield my carry-on, as I whizz past the masses amassed at the luggage carousel, watching the empty conveyor belt move like a Möbius strip in and out of the cavern that's supposed to produce suitcases. Robin said there would be a limo to pick me up, so I look for someone holding a placard with my name. Nobody. The arrivals sign clock says it's just past midnight. Probably way after quitting time for whoever was supposed to be here to ferry me to the hotel. I guess I'm on my own.

The lobby is deserted when the cab drops me off at the Gaylord Palms hotel an hour later. I trundle my bag to the front desk and am relieved when the desk clerk successfully finds my name on the list of rooms reserved for the conference. She hands me a keycard and points me toward a bank of glass elevators.

The Gaylord takes its relationship with palms very seriously. The carpet that greets me when I get off on the fourth floor is awash in bilious green fronds on a marine blue background. I hope this choice of décor doesn't extend to the rooms. I open the door to room 405. Then I double-check the cardboard sleeve that held my key. Yup, 405. The carpet pattern does indeed extend into the room. But that's not the worst thing about room 405. Despite the no smoking sign on the door, there's an ashtray full of butts in the middle of the unmade bed. The wastebasket holds several dead tequila bottles. The curtain rod is listing to the left. There's what looks like a pair of underwear on top of the lamp that's on the bedside table.

I back out of the room, taking care not to encounter any surfaces, and let the door close behind me. Good thing I only touched the outside doorknob. I drag my stuff back downstairs. I don't even need to fake looking pathetic when I approach the front desk and slap my key on the counter. "It's one thirty in the morning. I've been on the road since noon. The room you gave me isn't made up and is full of cigarette smoke and tequila barf. I have meetings starting at eight tomorrow morning. Or, actually, this morning. Can you just make me happy?" That last part was rhetorical. I don't think anything could make me happy at this moment.

The clerk types at her terminal, consults her screen and types again. "I'm so very sorry," she says. "IBM is a very good customer. I wouldn't want any of their employees to have a bad experience." She hands me a new key. I guess I work for IBM now. "Second floor. And have a nice day." Or more correctly, a rapidly dwindling night. Maybe they'll send up a fruit basket. Or a full bottle of tequila.

I haul everything back to the elevator. Even though I'm wearing my most travel-friendly shoes, my feet are killing me. I'm looking forward to changing into one of my many certified bomb-free pairs tomorrow. I don't want to walk any further today than from the elevator to room 222.

The door opens on a foyer with marble floors. There's a round table in the centre that holds a vase filled with pink lilies and white roses. No palm-infested carpet here. And so much for not walking any further. I'm looking at a hall that stretches as far as my blurry eyes can see. I first pass a dining room furnished with a table that seats eight, then a living room, which has two identical velvet couches, a glass coffee table, four leather lounge chairs that would enjoy being in the cigar smoking room of a fancy club (or come to think of it, the Sights Denim lobby), and an assortment of side tables. Even though my feet protest, I can't resist inspecting the wall of bookshelves filled with leather-bound volumes, spines lettered in gilt. I take one off the shelf. It's fake. Of course. But top marks for trying. I am in the land of Disney.

After that, there's a bathroom that looks larger than most apartments I've lived in. From the doorway, I can see a double vanity topped in white marble, a soaker tub as big as a plunge pool, and a walk-in shower that could house a herd of elephants. Then I finally arrive at the bedroom. Or at least to the foyer of the bedroom.

The bedroom has its own sitting room, another enormous bathroom, and a four-poster bed that looks like it could sleep seven people without even trying too hard. Red velvet curtains tied back with gold cords frame a window that overlooks an atrium, which is filled with palm trees (what else?), a babbling brook, and walkways that take guests back and forth from a pool and a bunch of restaurants. It would probably be uncharitable of me to go back downstairs and ask for a more private view.

I have my hotel routine well honed. I retrieve the luggage rack from its customary home in the closet, unfold it and put my carry-on bag on top. I take out my five pairs of shoes, line them up neatly on the floor of the closet, hang up my blouses, and place my suit on the valet stand. I put my bathroom stuff on the marble counter and play the usual game of where did they hide the hair dryer? It's extra hard in this bathroom, because there are many, many places it could be. The vanity has twelve drawers. There's also an armoire in the corner that probably used to belong to Louis XIV and could hide at least three dead bodies. Good thing I didn't leave this task for the morning. After a half-hour of lack of sleep I'll never get back, I finally find it behind a large rococo mirror that swings out to reveal a hair dryer–shaped niche in the wall. That's definitely a new one. I phone for a wake-up call at six o'clock. Four hours from now.

56

"Welcome to IBM ASP World 2001," says the woman at the registration desk. "I hope your accommodation is satisfactory." I nod affirmatively. I wonder if I've snagged the room of some senior executive who didn't show up. Maybe he'll get room 405 instead. Best not to mention the suite. She hands me a tote bag and a name tag. "All the conference materials are in there, along with your personal agenda. Don't forget we've got a private Bon Jovi concert on the last day! Your ticket's inside and also your invitation to a dinner with executives and VIP clients tonight at the El Plantain Cuban restaurant. The bus leaves from the front door at six. Oh. Here's Megan. She'll be looking after you."

A woman in a navy blue pantsuit and white dress shirt bustles up. She couldn't possibly look more IBM if she tried. "BDE! We're so glad to have you. I hope your room is comfortable." I tell her it's just fine. I neglect to add I've barely seen half of it. "Today we have you attending the sessions we've selected, including lunch with public relations staff, then dinner at one of the best Cuban restaurants in town. Then tomorrow you'll have your one-on-ones with the clients who'll tell their ASP success stories. Then there's a dinner at Disney World, then on the final day more one-on-ones and of course, the Bon Jovi concert. Let's get started, shall we?"

My exhausted feet struggle to keep up, as Megan jogs through the atrium like the Red Queen in *Through the*

Looking-Glass. Or the Blue Queen, in this case. "We don't want to be late for the opening plenary session! Wouldn't be good to have an empty seat staring back at Robert Redford." Robert Redford?

Megan leads me down a vertiginous auditorium aisle. I'm doing as dignified a version of old lady stair navigation as I can manage: one foot on the step, the other foot on the step. Repeat. This is partly because of the shoes I thought would be perfect and aren't, but mostly because the height could go span-to-span with a Pittsburgh bridge and not bat an eye. I'm pretty sure I'm going to free-fall down to the stage and take out Robert Redford. Ha! As if Robert Redford's ever going to show up at an IBM conference.

I manage to stay alive long enough to reach a seat in the front row that has a tent card on it that says it's reserved. For me. Megan removes the card and motions for me to sit down. She takes the seat beside me. I take out my notebook and Megan does the same. Looks like Megan and I will be joined at the hip for the duration.

The auditorium lights go down and the stage lights go up to reveal two comfy chairs angled at each other, with a coffee table in between. Robert Redford's in one of them. So close he's in spitting distance. "That's Mr. Gerstner," Megan whispers. "He'll be at dinner tonight." What about Robert Redford? Megan doesn't seem to think he's as important as Mr. Gerstner.

"So, Lou," says Robert Redford. "What are we going to talk about today?"

"Well, Bob, I think our audience wants your thoughts about innovation. They're all on the bleeding edge of technological excellence. Our big blue wave of application service providers is what makes that happen."

I try to figure out what credentials Robert Redford has to be talking about innovation, but I soon give up and immerse myself in enjoying the view. He's almost a senior citizen but still isn't remotely hard on the eyes. No need to pay attention to what he's saying. Forget about Jon Bon Jovi, even though he's more age appropriate. This may be the highlight of my trip. Megan is scribbling frantically. Maybe I can borrow her notes.

After the morning session, Megan hustles us off to lunch. "You'll get to meet the rest of the PR team," she says. I'm not sure why I would want to meet the rest of the PR team, but I'm hungry.

The PR room has several IBM ThinkPads lined up along a wall and a few printers. There's a buffet of hot chafing dishes, some salads, and a row of typical hotel desserts that I know from experience look lots better than they taste. "We'll regroup in thirty," she says. "You can use any of the phones to call your office." I notice then there's a bunch of black Touch-Tones on a table at the back. All of them are in use. "The press hangs out here, too. You might have to wait a bit." Then, thankfully, she leaves me alone. I guess since I'm safely ensconced in the PR domain. Unable to get into trouble. I wonder where Bob's eating?

The afternoon is uneventful and supplies more information about IBM's ASP offerings than I'm sure even Mr. Gerstner would want to know. After the last session of the day, I'm looking forward to taking a nap. Megan looks at her watch and picks up her pace as we walk back to the rooms. "We're late. We have to leave for dinner. Can't leave Mr. Gerstner waiting." My feet escalate their complaints by several decibels as I follow her to my next obligation.

There are several vans lined up under the hotel's portico to take us to the restaurant. I'm guessing Lou will travel with his own limo and entourage, which I dearly hope includes Bob. I wonder if he's single. Bob, I mean. Lou's far too old. Even if he's younger than Bob. Heck, I don't care if Bob isn't single. Megan and I get into the first van in the row. "Do you like Cuban food?" she asks. I don't mention the Atlanta sandwich, but any restaurant named after plantains does not bode well.

"I'm happy for any meal someone else cooks," I say. This seems to be a good response.

We're ushered into a private dining room with several round tables. Lou is there. Bob is not. Megan and I are seated at the back of the room. I guess BDE isn't as important as I thought. No matter. Free food!

Megan chit-chats about living in Orlando, while I peruse the set menu. It's all in Spanish. I don't speak Spanish and, strangely, although they are cousins, Spanish food names seemingly have no relationship to French ones. *Ropa Vieja. Arroz con Frijoles Negros. Lechon Asado.*

"What's your favourite Cuban dish, Megan?"

"I love a Cubano sandwich," she says. "But not tonight. I think I'll have the lechon." She neglects to tell me what that is. And I don't ask. Megan resumes her monologue — about working in PR, about working for IBM, about how exciting it is to be in the room with Mr. Gerstner. Confirming that, in her view, Robert Redford doesn't rate.

When the waiter comes by, I tell him my four-course choices and hope for the best. Lou gives a welcome speech while we wait for our dinner. It involves giving ourselves a round of applause for IBM's great success at raking in the ASP bucks and something about being the most innovative company in the world. But not as innovative as Robert Redford, evidently.

57

I have no idea what I'm eating, except I do recognize the plantain at twenty paces, hive it off to my side plate, and substitute my salad fork for my dinner fork, just in case. Megan's too busy filling me in on the benefits of getting your kids into a good daycare spot to notice. Lou doesn't notice either. He seems to have had an entirely different menu that involves prime rib carved at the table. At this point, I'm way past exhausted.

"Megan, I have a big day tomorrow. Is it possible I can sneak out? Maybe take a cab back to the hotel?" Megan looks horrified.

"Oh. Of course! We need you totally on your game tomorrow. I'll get a van for you right away." She produces a walkie-talkie from thin air and pages my ride. "I'll come with you. He should be here in a sec." We grab our ride in front of the restaurant. "Did you enjoy the dinner?" I tell her I was happy to be there. No need to mention the food. It's about a forty-mile drive back to the hotel. At about mile two I start to feel queasy. Could be just the bumpy ride, I'm hoping. Not the plantain.

When we get back to the Gaylord, I say a brusque farewell to Megan and manage to not barf before agreeing to meet her at the PR room for breakfast at eight. I race to the elevator, hand over my mouth, determined to get to one of my spacious bathrooms before my dinner comes back up.

Which isn't possible, given the expanse of foyer between me and the facilities. The marble floor sustains collateral damage as I lurch toward the toilet. I curl up on the bathmat and wait for more intestinal revenge. Which does not disappoint. I resume my earthbound horizontal position. I never realized a bathroom floor could be so cozy. When you have no choice.

The next thing I hear is the phones ringing, telling me it's time to wake up. Redundant, since I'm pretty sure I've been up all night. Exuding noxious, chunky fluids from both the north and south ends. The happiest place on earth, indeed. I briefly lament losing the chance to wear my fabulous shoes, before succumbing to much deeper despair. Probably no Jon Bon Jovi either.

When I next wake up, I have no idea what time it is. Or even what day it is. I'm thankful I put the "do not disturb" sign on the door, otherwise I'm sure the maid would have been knocking every hour. I vaguely recall the phones ringing and ringing and ringing for a long time. But now they're silent. The good news is I'm pretty sure I've barfed up everything that was available in my stomach. The bad news is I'm also pretty sure I've missed the entire conference. And all my case study appointments. And totally pissed Megan off.

This morning — afternoon? night? — I finally feel capable of crawling out of the bathroom to the bedroom, avoiding getting too vertical, in case it might elicit new intestinal distress. I hoist myself up on the untouched bed and sprawl on the bedspread, having no choice but to ignore the warnings about the most unsanitary place in any hotel room. Actually, the joke's on them. I'm currently the most unsanitary place.

The message light on the phone beside the bed is flashing. Of course. I take a deep breath, which makes it abundantly clear I have not showered in three days, and press play.

Megan here. Still waiting for you at breakfast. Maybe our lines got crossed? Meet me at the PR room.

Megan here. Did you have other appointments I wasn't aware of? Page me please.

Megan here. We're waiting in the Plantain Room to start the case study interviews.

Megan here. Tried to stall the clients but they're getting mad.

Megan here. I didn't think BDE would be so unreliable and unprofessional. After all we did to facilitate your meetings. I'm calling Simon to ask him to explain himself.

58

Ricky is relaxing on the neighbour's porch furniture when I get home. He leaps over the railing, looks up with what I interpret as an adoring gaze, and stretches his paws up on the door. At least he hasn't forsaken me. I undo the lock and make my way through to a kitchen that for once doesn't smell like old cat food. I'll have to buy Greg a bottle of wine. And maybe hire him as my housekeeper.

The flashing message light dares me to reveal who's called me while I was away. I do not pick up the gauntlet. Instead, I examine the contents of the fridge, which unsurprisingly displays the same inventory as when I left, but three days sadder. I take a notepad out of the junk drawer and start making a list.

When I'm done with compiling the grocery order, Ricky follows me as I take my suitcase up to the second floor and put it on my bed. The red fabric of the carry-on is streaked with black marks from its travels through grubby airports and there's a small rip in the zipper. I guess it wasn't completely up to the three-month aviation marathon. There are probably suitcases specifically made for frequent flyers that you need a secret password to buy. A secret password that has yet to be revealed to me, despite my warrior wounds. Or maybe what you have to do is just flash your loyalty cards. I will likely never know.

I take my unworn shoes out of one half of the case. When I start to put them back in the walk-in closet, I realize I have a whole bunch of red shoes. Shouldn't the red ones all be grouped together? And the blue ones? And the black ones? Maybe they should be arranged by colour and hue. I spend a happy half-hour of denial perfecting my shoe-scape. When I stand back to admire my impeccably organized closet, I notice it's not *that* impeccable. I've got pants hung between dresses, jackets hung between blouses, and several skirts have escaped the tiered skirt hanger. Ricky is now relaxing in the side of the carry-on vacated by the shoes. At least it can have a life beyond its now defunct travel duties. A cat bed that will forever remind me of the dismal end to this project and probably my career in general.

After the closet has been transformed into a space worthy of a designer label showroom, I move up to the third floor. My desk is cluttered with pieces of paper and file folders. I dump the contents of my laptop bag on top of the pile and a fridge magnet falls out of my notebook. It's in the shape of a flamingo, sparkly pink except for the yellow "Florida" written in italic script across the flamingo's nether regions. I used to like flamingos. I had a pair of plastic ones between the panes of the window facing the street when I lived in an apartment over a store. I thought I was incredibly hip and funky. When I didn't yet know how my forty-something life would turn out. I throw the flamingo into the wastebasket beside the desk. No need to remind myself.

I busy myself writing labels for file folders, sorting pages into categories, tossing the discards into a pile for the recycling bin. I crumple a scrap of paper into a ball and toss it at Ricky, who has come upstairs to see what's going on. He ignores the makeshift toy and complains that it's past dinner time. "That guy that was feeding me wasn't this negligent," his cat whine says. He's right. The sun is way past the yardarm. But that means I'll have to go downstairs to the blinking red light.

Ricky continues to express his deep disappointment with my choice of priorities as I arrange the folders in the small filing cabinet that fits under the table, put pens back in the *Cathy* mug that says, "I love my career," and give the desk surface a swipe with the sleeve of my shirt. Nothing more to do here. Unfortunately.

Back in the kitchen, once Ricky's culinary needs have been dealt with, I take a deep breath, press play on the answering machine, and close my eyes, somehow thinking that will shield me from whatever is about to hit the fan.

Hey! It's your team calling. Are you coming out to NTN on Tuesday? Do you even exist?

Beep.

We did full diagnostics on the AC unit we took from your house and there's nothing wrong with it. Must be some other problem. Maybe your electrical panel needs upgrading. And maybe I'm an endless source of funds, Mr. HVAC guy. I try to remember what the electrician said about the wiring, other than needing to replace the knob and tube, and draw a blank.

And that's it for the messages. I'm not surprised there's nothing from Simon. I didn't really expect to hear from him. And why would I call him? To get yelled at? To get an "I'm appalled at your lack of professionalism" speech? I've probably wrecked the whole project. IBM's a major sponsor. We're still at least three case studies short of meeting BDE's obligation to them. What if they don't pay? Wait, even worse, what if I don't get paid? At the very least, I'll never get one of these contracts again.

59

"Nothing wrong with my wiring," I say when I call the HVAC guys back. This may or may not be true, but how are they going to know? "Must be something else. Maybe you should come and test the other components." It probably helps that I haven't paid the bill yet, because they promise to be here tomorrow.

Everyone's in their usual spot when I get to Scotland Yard for NTN night. Josh's t-shirt du jour says "sarcastic," spelled out using entries in the periodic table: sulphur, argon, calcium, sulphur, titanium, and carbon.

"Very clever, Josh," I say. "Easy way to remember elements. Maybe there'll be a chemical symbol round tonight."

"I sense you're really calling it ridiculous. Not as ridiculous as that project you're on. Is it done yet?"

"I don't know. I think so. But maybe not."

"How could you not know?" says Len. "Isn't it either done or not done? Should be as simple as a status meeting. Done or not done. Which is it?"

"Long story. I'll tell you later," I say, and deflect further interrogation by fiddling with my Playmaker to ready it for the game. Nobody would dare interfere with essential preparations for battle.

The warm-up is a cakewalk and we bag the full points. We pretty much always rule the bar, but that's not our objective. Our objective is to rate in North America, which can't happen until after the Category round. Howard is up on the mathematical machinations that dictate this reality. "Warm-up is pablum. Any newbie could make their way through that. Countdown is table stakes. Starts to separate the wheat from the chaff. Category is where our horses can start to own the track." Dubious metaphors aside, Howard is correct. If we miss the full spoils for the Category questions, we will not rate.

And now they are revealed by the screen. The choice is geography or history.

"Well, geography is pretty much static. How much can it change? History, on the other hand, is always being made. We have no way of knowing whether it'll be ancient or modern. European or North American. Guns or ploughshares," says Len.

"Len's right. And we're running out of time to vote. Let's go geography," says Josh.

We each key in our choice and await the question. As always, there will be five possible answers, with the point value diminishing as the choices disappear. My fingers are in their ready position on the numbers at the top of the Playmaker keyboard.

> Which of these is called a "tristate area" in the United States?
>
> a) New York, Pennsylvania, Delaware
>
> b) Colorado, New Mexico, Utah
>
> c) Washington, Oregon, Wyoming
>
> d) Indiana, Kentucky, Ohio
>
> e) Louisiana, Mississippi, Arkansas

Ha! I yell "team knows!" a little too enthusiastically but redeem myself by subtly showing the guys four fingers, as I confidently select Indiana, Kentucky, and Ohio. Then we wait for the update on the North America standings.

"Crap. The Borg's on top. A pox on those guys, whoever they are. But you're number two, Elvis." says Josh.

"I met them when I was in South Dakota! They're a bunch of douches. They do know their stuff, but I still won the bar. No fear, gentlemen. Stick with the tour. I can get inside their heads."

The Lightning round is sports, so we cruise through that, with me just a breath behind courtesy of my touch-typing reflexes. Then we're into the make-or-break pyramid question set. All of them need to be answered correctly to gain full points. We're doing pretty well until the final question:

> **This river was a primary transportation route for pioneers during the westward expansion of the early U.S.**

Surely, I know which river this is. We have five seconds until we have to answer. What was the river in Henderson? The Ohio. What was the river in Cincinnati? The Ohio. What was the river in Pittsburgh? The Ohio.

"Ohio," I stage whisper. "Ohio for sure."

I can imagine The Borg arguing about this one at length in their sad chlorine-scented bar. How would they even know what rivers are? I don't think South Dakota even has any. And just like that, my flaming fingers put me on the top of the North American rankings.

One more question to go. Final Strategy. "Don't mess up," says Howard. "Oh, I mean, let's not mess up. I don't want any of us to mess up. But especially not you."

"Bet it all, guys," I say. "I want to totally bury The Borg. My revenge is they can already see Elvis owns the house. They ain't nothin' but hound dogs."

The final question appears on the screen, with the list of possible answers.

If you land at ORD, which city are you in?

"Chicago," I mouth to my team. Then hold up two fingers. There's no way any of The Borg would know this. The most exciting place they've probably ever been is Sioux Falls. Or maybe Shreveport, if they're particularly adventurous.

Just for fun, NTN always takes an intermission before announcing the North American champions. "Okay," says Josh. "Spill the beer. What's up with the risky contract?"

"I don't recall that I ever called it risky. Just risk adjacent. So far, I've billed fifty-five thousand. American dollars. That's like a hundred million Canadian. Right, Len?"

"Yup. Pretty much. I admit that sounds okay. As long as they pay you."

"Well, I've billed them. And completed the work. Most of it, anyway."

"Most of it? Wait. Here are the standings!"

We look up to the screen above the fake fireplace. It says "Elvis" in flashing letters. I'm not even sure what you win when you win North America. Perhaps I should ask The Borg. But for now, we collect our free drinks and bask in the bar's applause.

"But I still don't get what's up with the status of your project," says Len. "Done or not done. Paid or not paid."

"There are mitigating circumstances," I say. "They involved the Norovirus. Lots of barf and other ejections of bodily fluids I will not discuss here. But right now, I have to get back to my cat. Unlike any of you, he actually missed me."

My bike helmet and I go off in a huff. I do not need more comments about my lack of steady employment. Nor helpful analysis of the current state of my HVAC renovations.

60

The HVAC guys have been mucking about for at least two hours. There's a swarm of them inspecting all levels of the house, blowing air through ducts, doing stuff with volt meters, and stomping up and down the stairs. The cat is not impressed. I let him out the front door and he immediately jumps over the railing to my neighbour's porch. I'm pretty sure he's planning to un-adopt me. Since he's not hogging my wicker chair, I sit outside and read the latest issue of *Toronto Life* magazine as I wait for some verdict on my faulty air-conditioning.

"The only thing it could possibly be is the thermostat," the guy that seems to know what he's talking about says. Turns out, the state-of-the-art technological marvel from Korea they told me would revolutionize my "home comfort experience" has been the problem all along. "We're out of stock on that one, though. Next overseas shipment should be here by the end of the month." He tries to look apologetic but fails when he looks at his watch, picks up his tool bag, and eyes the door.

"What are my options here? I'm still without the functional HVAC I was promised in the spring."

"I didn't want to suggest this for someone as fancy as you, but do you remember those round beige things your parents had on the wall? You just turn the dial to the temperature you want? But then you'll have to adjust it yourself if you want it up or down when you go to bed or you're out of the house," he says.

I convince him I'm capable of remembering to adjust the thermostat as required. And voila, I will have air-conditioning for the brief interval between today and the end of summer, but now I'll have to pay the balance of the HVAC bill. Plus, the cost of air-conditioning.

***

For once my machine has a worthwhile message.

Hey! Comment ça va! C'est Serge ici. Let's rendezvous this week. I have news.

"The day trading's been fine, but the technology market's still in the dumpster," says Serge when I meet him at one of our old haunts by the lake. Then he starts telling me about Normand's latest venture. Another tech company.

"I thought Normand was going sailing. Never working again."

"Well, his wife had a different idea. And so does mine."

"But another tech company? That dumpster's on fire!"

Serge is convinced this one is a winner. "It's called WebEx. Online video and audio conferencing. It's going to be huge. You can meet remotely and save travel costs. Plus, you can show PowerPoint slides and share documents. Once they get snapped up by a big player, we'll get rich on our stock options."

"If it was FedEx, I'd believe you. Are they trying to trick people into thinking they're associated with FedEx?"

"Just wait and see. This one's a winner."

We take our drinks to go and stroll along the lake shore to Yonge Street. The Toronto Star Building looms a few blocks away.

"Do they have an office in Toronto? The conferencing people?"

Serge shakes his head. "That's the point. Normand's opening one. At first, it'll be just corporate sales, but then there'll be tech support. That's what he wants me to do. Establish the tech support part. Maybe a data centre. Hey — I wonder if the space Maxlink had is still available?"

"Yet another reason why I wouldn't want to work there. I'd have flashbacks."

The sailboats are all out in the inner harbour and I can see the island ferries making their leisurely way from the mainland to the parks and beaches. I haven't been to the island even once this summer. Or anywhere else I usually go, for that matter. And it's almost Labour Day.

61

The thermometer still thinks it's high summer, even though my birthday's next week. It was always depressing to have a birthday on Labour Day weekend when I was a kid. Vacation's almost over. Back to the grind. Come to think of it, even more disappointing as a grown-up.

I dutifully embark on a run, starting out already drenched in sweat from the tropical air. But at least it gets me out of the house, and I don't have to think about anything. Like causing the implosion of an important project and my ballooning line of credit.

Ricky's sprawled on the concrete walkway when I return, trying to get some relief from the heat. He's not yet caught on to the concept of air-conditioning, but I certainly have. That's one good thing: the consolation of coldness when I open the door. The answering machine blinks, as usual. The phone only rings when I'm not there. It's probably people wanting to clean my ductwork (my brand new, gold-plated ductwork) or reshingle my roof (my brand new, gold-plated roof).

I do everything I can possibly do before pressing play. Gather the trash for garbage day. Check the grocery inventory. Throw in a load of laundry. Clean the bathroom shower. Transfer the laundry to the dryer. Alphabetize my spices. Memorize the current names of all the countries in Africa. I don't actually get to that last one, but it's on my list. Surely one of these days countries in Africa will be the final NTN question. Because it was good luck before, I close my eyes before instructing the answering machine to let me have it.

Hi! It's Holly! Um, have you heard from Simon lately? I don't know if the project's done or not. Should I be scheduling more interviews for you? Think we were supposed to wrap up by the end of September. Call me back.

Beep.

Robin here. I don't see any trips for you on the horizon, but I haven't heard from Simon in a while and his voicemail is full. If you talk to him, please tell him my invoice hasn't been paid.

This is a little odd. Surely Simon isn't mad at them too. Maybe he got fired because of the IBM disaster. No, scratch that, it was me. He got fired because of me. Forget about my bread-bonfire at Maxlink, I'm now croutons. Fried in boiling oil.

I have nothing else left to do but go up to my office and figure out what's next. Aside from the customary layer of cat hair, my desk is pristine. The laptop awaits my agile fingers. The modem is asleep, but willing to rouse itself at any time. The mug of pens still promises to be half-full of ones that work. The cordless phone stands at attention in its cradle, ready to intercept any and all calls, however unimportant.

The chair complains a little when I sit, rebuking me for my absences, or, more likely, lamenting the end of its extended vacation. *Don't you dare add your problems to the list of my problems*, I tell the chair. *My problem buffer is full.* I do a few twirls, just to annoy it, but the joke's on me because now I'm dizzy.

What to do now? I open the filing cabinet and admire my organizational handiwork. The Orlando debacle is in a lovely purple folder. Just to torment myself further, I take it out of the drawer. I realize I've never really reviewed my interview schedule in detail, what with being extremely occupied in the bathroom for the duration. It's right there in the sheaf of papers I've carefully filed: the list of companies I was supposed to talk to.

Just for fun, and because the company names don't reveal very much about what they do, I summon the internet and type the first name into Dogpile. It appears that Lexmark is a manufacturer of home-office printers, recommended for use with IBM PCs. No surprise there. Burlington Coat Factory isn't really a coat factory, but a discount clothing retailer in the Midwest. Artisan and Truckers Casualty Company turns out to be a regional insurance company, which isn't too unexpected, but specializing in artisans and truckers is definitely a unique niche. Finally, Popstroke. This is a chain of mini-putt golf courses in Utah. Mormon mini-putts. Who knew there were Mormon mini-putt magnates out there? However, none of this information is of use to me, although it did allow me to successfully kill an otherwise idle hour.

I pick up the page from my desk to refile it. Then I notice it also includes contact names and phone numbers for the people I was scheduled to meet. I may have caused the IBM disaster, but maybe I can fix it.

62

Holly's machine intercepts my call. "Hi Holly. No, I haven't heard from Simon, but we didn't exactly get the interviews done at the IBM conference. Long story. Maybe you can reschedule them as phone meetings for me? As far as I know we need to wrap this up ASAP and won't have the time to travel." That last part is kind of fictional, but if you squint, it'll look real enough to most people.

The four companies I need to interview are all over the U.S.: Utah, Mississippi, Iowa, and Kansas. I'm kind of disappointed I won't get to go to Kansas because maybe they'd have a fridge magnet shaped like Dorothy's red slippers, but there's no way I can foot the airfare and hotel bills. Nothing to be done until Holly gets back to me. Might as well go to the gym.

***

Hi! It's Holly. Happy to book phone interviews for you. Just email me the details and I'll get right on it. No surprise that the phone rang while I was in spin class. But good news that Holly will be on the case. For a change, I've got work to do.

I peel off my smelly gym clothes, quickly pull a t-shirt dress over my stringy hair, and head up to my office. Ricky expresses his unhappiness as I shove him off the lid of my laptop, which must be much more comfortable to sleep on than it looks. "There's a perfectly good carry-on in the bedroom," I tell him. "And there's tuna water in the kitchen." The anticipation of fishy ambrosia seems to perk him up and he thumps down the third-floor stairs, leaving a tumbleweed of cat hair behind him.

As I wait for the modem to connect, I muse about the benefits of working from home. I don't need to worry about looking presentable because nobody can see me. Nor can their email see me. I could be in my pyjamas, for all they know. Except I don't wear pyjamas, which would be taking things a little too far. I type the IBM interview info into an email and send it off to Holly. And cross my fingers. I don't bother changing my clothes before I head out on my bike to Scotland Yard. My helmet hair will complement my sweat-stained dress. And the guys won't notice anyhow.

***

Today's questions are not going our way. We limp through the first three rounds, getting more discouraged with each flubbed answer. At this rate we won't even win the bar. Next up is the Category round. It's history or geography again.

"I repeat my sage advice: history is a slippery devil. Geography has its feet firmly on the ground," says Josh. His t-shirt today says "T-Shirt" on the front.

Which of these is the capital of Burkina Faso?

"Yes! Slam dunk on this one. You know all the African capitals right?" Len points to me.

"Ummm. Not exactly."

"I thought you were going to memorize them. It was one of your New Year's resolutions. From like seven months ago.

Don't you have lots of time on your hands these days? What's the delay?"

"No point in doing that now. African capitals aren't likely to show up again any time soon. Anyhow, I have more important things to do," I say.

"Like what? Alphabetizing your spice rack?" says Howard. I give him the finger. And fail to mention I've already done that.

Turns out the answer is Ouagadougou. At least I have now memorized one capital. Better late than never.

We continue to embrace our losing streak and end up with a pittance to bet on the final Countdown. The last question comes up on the screen:

> Which of these is the well-known nickname for Shreveport?

"Weren't you just there?" says Josh.

"A month ago, but I didn't even stay overnight. I have no idea what its nickname is. Well-known my ass. Probably should be something to do with noxious hot dogs and pickup trucks with gun racks. Hey — I could write a country song and make a million dollars! On the plus side, did I tell you my air-conditioning finally works?"

"Cut the chit-chat. Here're the answer choices."

Our options are:

> a) Ratchet City
>
> b) Las Vegas South
>
> c) The Oil Well
>
> d) Ark-La-Tex
>
> e) Steamboat Willie

"It did start out as an oil town and there's a lot of gambling. But Steamboat Willie was a Disney character. Precursor for Mickey Mouse. It's not that one," I say.

"Dude, we all know about Steamboat Willie. We just don't know about Shreveport. You should be more help than this," Len says.

"I'd go with b or c. Toss a coin. And I'm not a dude, in case you've never noticed. Believe me, life would be easier if I were. Or at least my travel wardrobe would be."

With a couple of seconds to spare, Josh says, "Las Vegas South. And because it's Las Vegas, let's bet it all. Let the good times roll. Wait, that's the motto for New Orleans. Never mind."

"Ratchet City? Who the shit has ever heard of Ratchet City?" Josh says when the answer is revealed. Then there's the customary pause before the standings appear. "The Borg. The Borg fucking knows what Ratchet City is. A pox on them! No, a stoat on them! Rip out their lungs!"

"Told you they were a bunch of dickheads," I say.

"Nerdheads is more like it. So, what's the status of your project? Done or not done?" says Josh, who has disavowed any responsibility for our total shutout.

"I don't know. Working on it. Might be done soon, unless it already is."

"Sure wouldn't want to be your project manager. What would I put in the status report? Um, not sure? Will let you know when I know?"

"I have a plan. Just in the process of executing it." Unless I'm the one who gets executed. "Status report next week. It will be done or not done or in the process of being done."

63

Holly's disembodied voice fills my kitchen.

Hi! It's Holly! The good news is I've reached the IBM ASP case study candidates and they're still willing to be interviewed. The bad news is all but one of them refuses to do a phone interview because, as the coat guy said, "it'll be like a consolation prize." That mini-putt guy said he wanted us — meaning you — to really experience his business. Play a few holes. Eat some hot dogs. Pretty weird, huh?

This is not good. This is not even good adjacent. The deadline I've set for myself is the interviews must be finished and written up by the first week in September. A deadline that's showing all signs of being dead in the water. The only sensible thing to do at this moment is have lunch.

My cupboard tells me I'm down to my last can of tuna, which I hope only means I'm down to my last can of tuna, not my *last* can of tuna — ever — because I'll be a bag lady by the end of the month.

I tug on the drawer that harbours the can opener. It opens about half an inch and will not budge. I slide my right hand into the abyss and encounter a wooden handle. Definitely not the can opener. I slide my hand to the left and let my fingers do the walking over the undifferentiated utensils, like a blind chef. Only I am neither skilled at being blind nor at being a chef.

"F—ing hell!" My innocent index finger finds the tip of the corkscrew. Can you open a can with a corkscrew? I don't know. But clearly, you can open a finger. Wounded but not daunted, I slide my left hand into the abyss and explore the top side of the drawer. The potato masher! The potato masher is angled so that it prevents the drawer from budging. I try to recall when I last used a potato masher. Maybe that's also what the potato masher's doing. Making sure I remember I own a potato masher.

I give the drawer an ultimatum. Either it goes or I do. Then I wonder if that was wise. What happens if it wins? And how stupid is having a conversation with a drawer? About as stupid as my situation in general, I am forced to admit.

I wiggle my left hand out of the drawer, pleased to see it's mostly intact except for bruised knuckles. I withdraw my other hand, and the drops of blood ooze out to the front of my favourite workout shirt. I grab the drawer on either side and give it a whack. This magically dislodges the potato masher enough that I can reach the can opener. I eye the masher with murderous intent, but I'm distracted by Ricky, who's emerged like a genie from his cat allergen–infested hiding place du jour. *Tuna water*, his feline tuna detector says. He's currently the only one in the house who's happy with his lot.

As a sad looking English muffin defrosts in the microwave, I mix up a minimalist filling of tuna and mayonnaise. There aren't even any wilted lettuce leaves languishing in the crisper and the cucumber has long ago devolved into green ooze. Much like my life. I arrange my pathetic sandwich on a plate, along with a flaccid dill pickle, tuck a can of Perrier under my armpit and trudge up the stairs to my office to contemplate my next steps.

All of the unanswered questions are out there, swirling around my attic, and soon they're joined by Ricky who's likely been summoned by cat ESP to my half-eaten tuna sandwich. I pry apart the sides of the muffin and put the plate on the floor as an open-faced feline buffet. And continue to ruminate. How do I do interviews that aren't in person and make them kind of feel like they're in person? How do I get all this done in ten days or less?

I distract myself from my imminent prospects of self-immolation by doing a few chair twirls. Clockwise. Counterclockwise. Clockwise. Counterclockwise. Wait. What did Serge say? Online conferencing? Something to do with FedEx? I pick up the phone.

Of course I get his machine. What did we do before answering machines? *Actually* answer the phone? "Serge, it's me. I have a proposition for you. It would help us both out. Well, actually, it would probably help Normand out too. But we'd have to move fast. Call me back as soon as you can."

I have no idea when Serge might call back, so I have no intention of venturing too far from my phone. I take the remains of my cat-mauled lunch downstairs and dump it in the garbage. I grab the cordless handset from the kitchen, scoop up the *Toronto Life* magazine from the front hall table, and go out to the front porch. Might as well enjoy a small sliver of the waning summer as much as I can. Which, in this moment, isn't very much. The phone remains stubbornly silent, as opposed to Ricky, who's asking me what happened to the rest of his tuna. I fling my magazine in his direction, or at least in the direction he used to be before he saw me lift the magazine, and I decide it's better to go for a run. Guaranteed Serge will call when I'm not here.

And I wasn't wrong. Serge's voice is on the machine when I get back.

What? A proposition? Should I tell my wife? Haha! Meet you at my new office tomorrow if you dare. Twenty-fourth floor, One Yonge Street. I think you know where that is. I'll be in by nine o'clock.

64

It's déjà vu when I secure my bike at the base of One Yonge Street. But now I have two locks: a Kryptonite U-lock that attaches the frame to the upright of the rack and a two-yard-long cable that threads through both wheels and snakes back to hook into the inside of the Kryptonite. Take that, evil thieves.

I feel a little creeped out as I walk through the familiar lobby. People are bustling toward the elevators with takeout cups of coffee, bantering with their colleagues about the Blue Jays' post-season prospects. They probably think I'm a bike courier, since I'm wearing workout clothes and carrying a pannier. No need to impress Serge or anyone else in this building.

A buzzer goes off when I open the office door into the unstaffed reception area on the twenty-fourth floor. The place looks pretty much the same as when I last saw it, an unwelcome blast from the past. I see Serge waving at me on the other side of the glass doors leading to the inner sanctum. I wonder if Normand now has Joel's old office space, and if Joel's old office really looks like a Vegas hotel suite, as was the Maxlink rumour du jour.

"I see you dressed up for the occasion!" I roll my eyes. Serge is clad in a pair of sweatpants and a freebie Jays t-shirt celebrating opening day 1999. "Come on into the boardroom. It's the only place that currently has internet in this joint. Ironic, isn't it? Considering Maxlink's mission to deliver internet to everybody. Anyhow, what's up?"

I remember the room for its panoramic view of the lake and at this time of year it doesn't disappoint. Sparkling water. Languid sailboats. I pull my notebook out of my pannier, click open my pen, and tell Serge the full saga of my past two weeks, omitting the details of the noxious-bathroom-in-the-fancy-suite escapade. "So, this WebEx thing. Could I do interviews online and have it be almost the same as in person?"

Serge almost upsets his Aeron chair as he leaps to his feet to go to the whiteboard. He flails around to locate a pen from the ledge that typically holds the writing implements, but there are none. "Damn you, Joel! Couldn't you even leave a scrap behind? There isn't even any toilet paper in the bathrooms!" I let him continue his rant as I zip open my pannier and throw him a dry-erase marker. If nothing else, I've learned to be prepared in my travels.

"Red. I was hoping for blue," Serge says.

"TFB," I say, as I lean back in the outrageously expensive office chair. "And I'm not even going to translate that Englishism for you. Translations are for winners, not losers."

He says something in French that sounds rude, then uncaps the pen and proceeds to draw a schematic to show how WebEx works. The hip bone connects to the thigh bone. The thigh bone connects to the knee bone. The knee bone connects to the leg bone. The leg bone connects to the ankle bone. Or something like that.

"Serge, that's a very nice drawing, but all I need to know is, can I use this WebEx thingy to connect to several people in the U.S. — not all at the same time — to a video conference call that'll last about three hours?"

"Yes! Didn't you hear what I was saying? Were you not paying attention?"

I am now. We're discussing logistics. Can I do it from this boardroom? Can Serge be my tech support? Is this idea insane? Yes, yes, and yes.

All parts of my bike are still there when I leave the building. It's a miracle. And so is WebEx. I now have a plan. Maybe not a good plan, but a plan, nonetheless. I stuff my pannier full of my bike anti-theft devices, attach its clips to my rat trap, and ride east to the Don Valley path that will take me home via steep and windy Pottery Road.

When I reach the bottom of the massive hill, I gear down as low as I can go and stand up to grind up the climb. I repeat my mantra as I pump my thighs to hamburger. *WebEx. WebEx. WebEx.* But when I can finally see the top, it's still too far to contemplate. I dismount, wipe my forehead with my forearm and walk my bike the remaining two hundred yards. Close. But close is not going to cut it.

As soon as I get home, once the sweat stops dripping into my eyes, I call Holly. "Holly," I say to her machine. "Let's start with the guy who'll commit to a phone interview. Only it won't be by phone, it'll be by WebEx, video conferencing that works over the internet. Ask him about Wednesday — any time between ten and two. I'll send you the link to give him. And we'll attach the interview guide as well." I can feel the ball moving forward. But Simon is still nowhere to be found.

65

Serge scurries about setting up the equipment we'll need. Which isn't much. My laptop and a larger screen that's on the wall of the boardroom. "That's optional," he says. "The point of all this is to web conference anywhere you want. Like from Normand's sailboat."

"So that's why he's so interested in the company," I say. "He can work from anywhere."

I dial in early for the call and open all the documents I'll need on the virtual desktop. A piece of useless trivia pops into my head unbidden. Apparently, when television was being demonstrated at the world's fair in 1939, people thought the image was pre-recorded, so they came up with the idea of pointing the camera toward the audience to show live pictures that couldn't possibly be recorded. Taking a cue from Serge's comment, I angle my laptop so my background is the view of the sailboats on the lake, with the rationale that it shows how versatile the technology is.

"You know," says Serge, "maybe we could use you as case study of our own. A case study about doing case studies remotely. Well, not really about case studies, but doing in-depth interviews, maybe."

I tell him I'll think about it. "Depends on how it goes. And will you pay me?'

"Who's letting you use WebEx for free?" He continues to itemize things I owe him for until I tell him to shut up because

Mack Klein from Artisan and Truckers Casualty has just appeared on my screen, looking exactly like an executive from Artisan and Truckers Casualty should look: a cross between someone who has a booth at the fall fair and someone who knows his way around a CB radio. I think the word "folksy" was invented just for Mack Klein.

I wave and gesture to my backdrop. "Nice day for sailing, here in Toronto."

"Toronto's on the ocean? And why are you in Toronto?" he says.

"No, it's on Lake Ontario, actually. And I'm here visiting one of our satellite locations. Because we use WebEx, we can conduct this type of interview from anywhere." I think I sound artisanal yet knowledgeable about my craft. As nice a combo as Mr. Klein has going on. In my opinion.

I can tell he's a little skeptical at first, but as we get to the meat of the discussion, he leans back in his chair and fiddles with a fountain pen, just like he'd probably do if the interview was in person. I extract the information I need for the case study, convince him to put some tangibles on the list of benefits, and gather lessons learned. It all takes less than two hours. And neither airport nor airport food was involved. I wrap up our session and let him know when to expect the draft of the case study to review.

"You know, I was a little annoyed we didn't do the interview when I was in Orlando, but this was actually much better. I had so many things to do when I was down in Florida. This way I could just insert it into my normal day," he says.

"Glad to hear that, Mack. I'm still trying to meet with the other guys we were supposed to interview at the conference. They're a little reluctant to do it by phone. Do you think they might like WebEx?"

"Hell yes! They'll probably be just like me and wonder why IBM doesn't have a technology like this."

"Would it be okay if I send a clip from our interview out to them? So they can see what it's all about?"

"Hell yes!"

And with that, I'm on the road to getting the other interviews done without actually going on the road.

66

The inevitable flashing light greets me in the kitchen when I get home. Probably not Holly and can't possibly be Robin since I'm not going anywhere. Maybe it's the HVAC guys? Or Josh? No, not Josh. It's already Thursday.

I've discovered it's much more fun to speculate who's called me than play the messages, so I don't just yet. Instead, I tidy up the kitchen, take my laptop and notebook up to my office, and start writing up the case study.

Ricky jumps up on the desk and scratches his cheek on the corner of my screen. And looks at me expectedly. I notice the sun's at the angle that, at this time of year, means it's past six o'clock and that it's time to pack it in for the day, if the cat has anything to say about it. I leave my work-in-progress on the table and go down to the kitchen.

The light's still flashing. Of course. I put some fresh food down for Ricky and press play. I don't even bother closing my eyes. It's probably somebody trying to sell me something.

Hi. It's Simon. I'm sorry I've been AWOL. I had the Norovirus then the entire house got the Norovirus, including the dog, and I had to look after them and I can't begin to tell you how bad it was. My voicemail filled up. My email filled up. And I'm only now wading through it. I didn't want to make you wait any longer because I'm sure there was a message from you somewhere in there. Anyhow, can you come to the office tomorrow? Friday? Around ten? I want to get caught up on the status. Haven't heard from IBM either. I was wondering—

Beep.

He gets cut off by the machine. An interesting turn of events, to say the least. Maybe all is not lost. Yet. I grab some yogurt from the fridge and head back up to my office. I want to get today's interview written up before my meeting with Simon.

***

"Got the IBM case study you sent," Simon says when I arrive at his office. "Haven't had a chance to look at it, but I'm sure it's fine. I've left several messages for Megan and now her voicemail is full. So, nothing to be done about that. How was Florida?"

I tell him the full story, leaving out the goriest parts of my stint on the bathroom floor. But he's had Norovirus, so he can fill in the blanks.

He laughs. "I know Norovirus isn't funny, but that story was funny. Bananas, even! Get the joke? And you missed Bon Jovi! I told you IBM had great private concerts. But wait. How did you get that case study done? Were you able to do it before you got sick?"

I explain about Holly helping out to arrange interviews with the candidates I was supposed to meet at the Gaylord. "You were right about not doing phone interviews," I say, hoping he still doesn't know about Augusta. "They much prefer to sit down with someone in person. It shows a certain level of interest." I press on. "But since nobody could get in touch with you to approve travel, we had to improvise. Have you heard of WebEx?"

"Of course I know WebEx. It's one of the companies we follow quite closely. At least the telecom guys do."

"Right. So, one of my previous colleagues is opening up the Canadian sales office and he suggested I might use it to do the interviews remotely. It would be a kind of proof-of-concept for them, and it would mitigate the lack of travel while still kind of being in person. Win–win."

"The Canadian analysts would be really interested in meeting with your colleague. Could you set that up?"

I tell him they'd be delighted to talk to an analyst firm. Serge had better be delighted. There couldn't possibly be more valuable PR.

"Win–win–win! I'll get in touch with IBM somehow and tell them we'll have the case studies completed by next week. And I'll let Holly and Robin know we're officially done."

I stand up to leave, thinking the meeting is over. But Simon's not finished yet. "Can you stay a bit longer? There's something I want to float by you. This project shows all the signs of being a huge cash cow."

Simon grabs a whiteboard pen as I sit back down.

"What do you know about business analytics?"

"Well, we had a business analytics practice at Brown & Associates, where I ran the information management group. We had to work pretty closely together. I'd say I know a little more than how to spell it, but not enough that you'd be able to bill me out at two thousand a day."

"We're getting into gear to do this all over again, only for business analytics. Same drill. Except this time, I'd like you to be the financial analyst as well. Tweak the methodology. Review everybody's spreadsheets. That's a thousand dollars for each case study, including the ones you do yourself, on top of the twenty-five hundred for the studies I'll earmark for you. Are you in?"

I take a few moments before I respond, pretending I'm examining the diagram he's drawn on the wall. Pretending my inside self isn't jumping up and down and saying *thirty-five hundred dollars! U.S.!* I do a quick calculation: fifty thousand, plus sixty-two thousand, five hundred. One hundred and two thousand five hundred! That's a hundred, eighty thousand Canadian. At least.

"Sounds like a great project, Simon. Can I get back to you on Monday? I've got some guys coming to the house about my HVAC. Have a nice weekend!"

I pick my bike helmet up from the floor and make my way down to the front of the building. I take it as a good sign when, once again, there are no visible bits missing from my bike. I feel a twinge of guilt for leaving Simon in limbo over the weekend. But only a very slight twinge.

I'll call him on Monday. After lunch. And ask him when we start.

www.ingramcontent.com/pod-product-compliance
Lightning Source LLC
Chambersburg PA
CBHW020228170426
43201CB00007B/356